I WAS NEVER HERE

My True Canadian Spy Story of
Coffees, Code Names and Covert
Operations in the Age of Terrorism

ANDREW KIRSCH

I WAS
NEVER
HERE

PAGE
TWO

Cataloguing in publication information is
available from Library and Archives Canada.
ISBN 978-1-77458-133-9 (hardcover)
ISBN 978-1-77458-134-6 (ebook)

Page Two
pagetwo.com

Edited by Pam Robertson
Copyedited by Jenny Govier
Proofread by Alison Strobel
Jacket design by Taysia Louie
Jacket photos by Michal García
Interior design by Fiona Lee
Printed and bound in Canada by Friesens
Distributed in Canada by Raincoast Books
Distributed in the US and internationally by Macmillan

22 23 24 25 26   5 4 3 2 1

andrewkirsch.ca

For Andrea, Benji and Eli

CONTENTS

INTRODUCTION

IT WAS 1:30 a.m. and I was sitting in the passenger seat of a full Dodge Caravan parked on a quiet residential street in the suburbs of Toronto. I was about to lead a covert special operations team to search the inside of the car of a suspected terrorist. The only catch: the car was parked in his driveway and he was sleeping at home with his wife and family.

It would end up being the longest night of my professional career as a spy with the Canadian Security Intelligence Service. That night everything that could go wrong would go wrong, but in the moment I didn't know that. All I knew was that I had a three-hour window to search this car before the sun started coming up and the neighbourhood began to stir. I also had a two-hour window to get home to my wife. She knew I was a spy and never asked where I was going when I left the condo at midnight in a dark hooded sweatshirt. She did like to know when I'd be home. The truth was I never really knew, but I got good at guessing. It was the least I could do. I think it helped her sleep, but if she woke up past the agreed upon time and I wasn't there, she'd really get worried. Operationally, "Don't get caught" was number one. "Don't upset my very understanding wife" wasn't far behind.

From my vantage point in the front seat, it didn't look good. There were a lot of people working that night. There was my team in the van. Surveillants were parked strategically throughout the neighbourhood, and one person back at the office was monitoring communications. The target in the house was an issue, but the more pressing concern was a neighbour who'd decided to walk his dog and have a smoke at 1 a.m.

I'd surveyed the neighbourhood to prepare for that night. I knew when garbage day was and when the last lights started to go off and the street quieted down. This was new, and it was really annoying. This insomniac dog walker was unknowingly interfering with a high-priority national security operation, and he was costing the government thousands of dollars in overtime pay. We were primed and ready to go. In the meantime, we were taking bets on how long it would take the dog to finish its business.

Stuck in a holding pattern, my mind drifted to the ridiculousness of it all. The pooping dog, our mission that night and the fact that I was responsible for leading it. We were about twenty-five minutes from where I grew up, and what I was about to do would be considered illegal if it hadn't been sanctioned by the government and authorized by a judge. It was a far cry from my previous career as a junior financial analyst at a bank in the UK.

I was part of a post-9/11 wave of civically minded Canadians who had left our day jobs to do our part in the age of terrorism. I had been in CSIS for about seven years and on the special operations team for a year. Even my first post as an analyst at headquarters felt like a lifetime ago. Back then I'd been chained to a desk reading reports and writing memos. It had been slow, but I'd been safe and anonymous behind the organization's walls and my air-gapped computer. My new role in special operations was the tip-of-the-spear stuff. It's what I'd signed up to CSIS to do. As always, sometimes be careful what you wish for.

The man and his dog had gone inside. The lights inside the house were off. The neighbourhood was quiet again. The chatter in the van died down as everyone began to re-focus and mentally prepare for what we were about to do. In the front seat I went back through my pre-operation checklist. Radio check. Phones on silent. Pockets empty of any identifying materials. Surveillance confirmed the perimeter was clear. At the same time everyone in the van checked and then rechecked their gear. They were now sitting quietly waiting for my command.

That was one of my first jobs in charge of an operation. I oversaw all aspects of the mission: plotting our objective, building a plan, procuring the tools we needed, getting the relevant approvals from management and then leading the team to achieve our goals. Most stages are a team effort and involve a lot of time, people and collaboration. However, when you execute a plan, it's not a democracy. The lead calls the shots. Most of the other guys had done hundreds of these operations. It could be intimidating and awkward to tell them what to do. But the reality is that if something happened, there wouldn't be time to have a group chat. A chain of command must be followed so everyone knows where to look for directions and instructions. Now they were looking at me.

I took a deep breath and gathered myself. There would be plenty of time to reflect and laugh at all of it when it was over. It should have been a ten-minute job. It ended up taking over two hours. If I had known, I would have quickly texted my wife and told her I'd be late. Instead, I called over my radio, "All teams, this is One. We're heading out." I turned to the guys sitting in the back of the van. "Let's roll."

I HADN'T always wanted to be a spy. I didn't watch spy movies growing up or dream about being James Bond. I knew about the CIA but never really considered that Canada had an intelligence service or thought about what they did. Prior to 2001, Canada's defining terrorist incident was the 1985 Air India attack. I was six years old. Intelligence wasn't something I'd thought much about until all of a sudden it was.

That was in 2005. I was living in London, England, and a coordinated bomb attack had just blown up a double-decker bus and a Tube station near my office. I was well into a promising financial services career, but now fighting terrorism started to mean a lot more to me than the markets. That's when I first googled, "How do I become a Canadian spy?" I wasn't recruited; it wasn't an accident and it certainly wasn't a passive act. I moved back to Toronto, applied online and went through a long and arduous process of psychological tests, interviews, role playing, background checks and a polygraph. I didn't exactly know what I was getting myself into, but

I studied and prepped hard for each stage. After fifteen months I got a phone call. It was the middle of the summer and I was living in Toronto. Could I report to Ottawa in September? Absolutely, I told them. What should I tell my family and friends? "Be discreet," was all they advised.

I left the Service in June 2016. This was also a relatively quick decision. I didn't leave angry and there wasn't one moment that pushed me out the door. Just as much as I knew when I wanted to join, I also knew when it was time to leave. The enthusiasm of serving my country gave way over time to the gruelling reality of being a spy. The bureaucracy, the late nights, the white lies and the relentlessness of it all wore me down. On my last day I handed in my badge, various IDs and building passes. I was escorted out of the office with nothing besides a promotional flyer for the next CSIS alumni benevolent society barbeque.

When I decided I wanted to apply to CSIS, I realized pretty quickly that there was little information available about what that actually meant. Since leaving, I've started to be open with people about where I worked and share my perspective on the organization, what it does and what it's like to work there. I realize there is certainly interest, even from people who aren't in the security community or considering it as a profession. This book is my contribution to the conversation. To explain to Canadians what it is their intelligence service does, day in and day out, and to try to describe how that affected my life—from the time I joined, moving from Toronto to Ottawa and back again, to the time I left. I dated women, then got married and started a family, while at the same time trying to conceal from most people where I worked—and even from my closest friends and family, who knew where I worked, what I actually did there. Now I'm able to share what it's like to work there. This book may dispel some of the mystique around spying. While I may not have been an international man of mystery, I am still extremely proud of the work I did and the small part I played in keeping Canadians safe.

We as a nation have a unique intelligence service with a diverse cadre of officers and support staff that punches above its weight. This is my story about what CSIS is and what it's like to be a Canadian spy—as much of it as I can share, as authentically as possible—from recruitment, to training, to life behind the desk, to knocking on doors, and then picking the locks and breaking in. I hope you find this book as I did my spy career: mostly fun, at times challenging, but ultimately rewarding.

1

THE WORLD'S SECOND-OLDEST PROFESSION

WE SHOULD probably start before the beginning. You may have some familiarity with the Canadian Security Intelligence Service, but please allow me to provide some background in case you don't, and maybe even dispel some misconceptions that are out there. First things first, the Canadian Security Intelligence Service is also known as CSIS (pronounced see-sis). People who work there often refer to it colloquially as "the Service," which is actually a pretty cool nickname for an intelligence service, in my opinion.

Spying has often been referred to as the second-oldest profession in the world, but CSIS is a relatively new organization. It was founded by an act of Parliament in 1984. Its roots, however, date back to the 1970s and allegations that its predecessor, the Royal Canadian Mounted Police Security Service, used illegal investigative techniques during the Front de libération du Québec (FLQ) crisis. A federal royal commission known as the McDonald Commission was formed in 1977 and issued a final report in 1981. Its main recommendation was to separate intelligence collection from policing and create a civilian intelligence agency. And thus, Canada's domestic security intelligence service was born.

It is important to note that Canada does not have a separate foreign intelligence service. Some countries assume that we do and we're just incredibly covert. But alas, we're not *that* good. And as a result, there is no direct equivalency with the United States, to which we are most often compared. This can be confusing. The Central Intelligence Agency (CIA) works almost exclusively outside of the United States. Its mandate is to collect foreign intelligence relating to the political or economic activities of foreign states. CSIS can only collect foreign intelligence in a limited capacity within Canada (well, there are some exceptions, but they aren't worth getting into here).

Ah, you must be thinking, so CSIS is more like the FBI. Not really. The Federal Bureau of Investigation (FBI) is a domestic security service but also a law enforcement agency that investigates and prosecutes crimes. They more closely align with our Royal Canadian Mounted Police (RCMP). Whenever there is a terrorism or national security arrest, you will see it's the RCMP laying the charges. In many cases, the information that may have started the investigation was uncovered by CSIS. However, as CSIS does not have an enforcement mandate, they will pass that information to the RCMP, in a very limited and controlled manner, so the Mounties can start their own investigation and ultimately prosecute. (And if you are interested in that process, there are many legal and academic papers written about the intelligence-to-evidence challenge of information sharing between CSIS and the RCMP.)

A better understanding of CSIS can be found by looking at our British and Israeli counterparts. The British have two intelligence services. Domestically, the British have the Security Service, otherwise known as MI5. Separately, the British have a foreign intelligence service known as MI6, the Secret Intelligence Service. MI6 is famously James Bond's employer. Bond gets to travel the globe, foiling international terror plots and seducing women in nearly every country he visits. MI5 obviously does very important work too, but I think their equivalent fictional character is Rowan Atkinson's bumbling spy Johnny English. That's got to be tough for recruitment. Do you want to be like Daniel Craig or Mr. Bean? In this analogy Canada is Mr. Bean, which actually does kind of fit.

Israel has this distinction too. The Mossad is responsible for foreign intelligence and covert activities abroad, while the Shin Bet is responsible for internal security in Israel. As much as these organizations may have different geographic areas of interest and responsibility, they must work very closely together. Threats originating abroad may aim to attack closer to home. Any coverage gaps between the two organizations could have disastrous consequences.

In Canada, we have one organization, and it's responsible for covering the globe while operating largely domestically. If that sounds like a tough job, well, it is. We benefit greatly from information sharing with countries around the world and especially close relationships with key allies that are members of the Five Eyes community of countries. In addition to Canada, this group is composed of the United States, the United Kingdom, Australia and New Zealand. We share a broad range of signals, military and human intelligence in what is the world's closest intelligence-sharing network. Canada definitely contributes to this arrangement, but clearly we are one of the smaller players, and our absence of a foreign service does mean in some cases that we rely heavily on our partners for information.

Once again, there are lots of legal and academic papers debating whether we need a separate foreign service or have enough powers under the existing mandate to do what we need to do to keep Canadians safe. I'm sure that in some bureaucrat's bottom drawer in Ottawa there even exists a detailed plan of what it would take to establish our own Canadian MI6 or Mossad. Personally, I think things work fine the way they are, even though it did take me three pages to explain it all.

9/11 and 7/7: My Postgraduate Education

If that quick summary was all new to you, don't worry. There will be no quiz and you don't need to know any of that to understand the rest of my story. Truth be told, I honestly didn't know any of that stuff before I started looking into becoming a spy. And I certainly didn't back in September 2001. I was twenty-two years old and a few weeks into my senior year at Brown University.

Despite growing up in Toronto, my parents had spent a year at graduate school at Rutgers and fell in love with the US college experience. They encouraged my brothers and me to look at American schools for our undergraduate degrees. Brown is an Ivy League school, famous for its Open Curriculum, and the campus in Providence, Rhode Island, was the exact type of environment they wanted for us. For the purpose of this book, the most interesting thing to note about my experience at Brown is probably that my freshman orientation group leader was John Krasinski, who would go on to a very successful TV and movie career (coincidentally playing fictional spy Jack Ryan). Fans of John might be interested to know that all through university he was putting in his ten thousand hours, performing in improv comedy shows and going for professional auditions. Meanwhile, I was studying public policy and had no idea what I wanted to be when I grew up.

The morning of September 11, 2001, I was at home in the rented house I shared with six of my friends near the main university campus. The television happened to be on CNN as we were getting up and getting ready for our day. I remember the first reports of a plane hitting one of the twin towers. It was confusing more than alarming. Terrorism just wasn't prevalent or even conceivable. I was still a student living in a bubble. The thought of an attack on the United States wasn't something anyone worried about or considered at the time. The moment definitely registered—we just didn't know what it was or what it meant. We kept watching, and were trying to better understand what happened, when the second tower was hit. We were still watching when eventually the two towers crumbled to the ground.

In the following years, terrorism seemed to be everywhere: 2002, the Bali bombing; 2003, bombings of compounds housing Western workers in Saudi Arabia; 2004, the Madrid bombings and the Beslan hostages. War with Iraq was coming. The Canadian Forces began to enter Afghanistan, progressively ramping up operations. Terrorism was always there, and the Great Game of foreign conflicts in Afghanistan certainly wasn't new, but it was all new for me.

During those years, I watched the world change from London, England. As a Canadian in a post-9/11 world, it was hard to stay in the United States without a work visa. However, as a member of the Commonwealth I was able to apply to the United Kingdom for a working holiday visa that would allow me to live and work in the UK for up to two years. I thought it was a better plan than moving back to Toronto and in with my parents. So after graduating in 2002, I moved to London and ended up getting a job as a junior investment advisor with Anglo Irish Bank in a new wealth management division of what was primarily a commercial property lending bank. I had a return ticket to Canada booked for six months out. I stayed with Anglo for three years and took all the exams that were required by the Financial Services Authority to be regulated to give financial advice in the UK. As a side note, Anglo would be nationalized in 2009 (to be clear—after I left and not my fault) at the height of the global financial crisis.

In 2005, Anglo was still the darling of UK and Irish finance, and I had a bright future as a private banker. That was until events conspired to change my path in life. My father passed away suddenly in January. Then, on July 7 of that year, a coordinated bombing attack in the heart of London hit very close to where my brother (who was also in London at the time) and I were working. It was the catalyst I needed to make a change. Four years earlier, 9/11 had happened a few states away from where I was living at that time. Now, on 7/7, the bombs were going off down the street.

I was going through the motions at work. It was a good career and they treated me well. I had put in two years and countless hours studying to earn my investment advisor certification. Deep down I knew it wasn't what I wanted to be. I once told my faculty advisor that I thought I'd go to law school even though I didn't want to be a lawyer. He told me, "People don't go to carpentry school if they don't want to be a carpenter." Now I was studying to be a banker and didn't want to be a banker. Each morning I'd read the news with one eye on the financial pages and the other on the latest developments in the global fight against terrorism. My father's life being cut short made me look around and really consider where I was and what I was doing with mine. There was something bigger happening in the world. I felt I had something to contribute, and I wanted to do my part. I didn't know anything about the military or spying, but in my mind, those were the two ways to get on the front line of the fight against terrorism. I started researching what little I could find. It sounded good. It felt important, and with my father's death, it started to feel more urgent.

I moved back to Toronto and applied to join CSIS and the Queen's Own Rifles of Canada (QOR), a Canadian Army Reserve infantry unit. I didn't really know what either meant at the time (or that I would be accepted to into both). I was ready to serve my country and do more with my life. I was young, restless in my career and itching to contribute. The army felt like a noble way to serve and a more realistic goal. CSIS seemed more like a pipe dream. They receive thousands of applications a year for only a handful of spots. I knew if I got in I'd have to move to a new city and potentially lie to people about where I worked and keep from those closest to me what I did there. I'd deal with all the life-changing stuff later. The hardest part at that point was just getting in.

2

THE LONG ROAD OF RECRUITMENT

S O HOW does one become a spy? That's the question I get asked the most. What is the process like? The short answer is, I applied online. I wish it were a cooler answer; unfortunately, it isn't. I didn't know anyone who worked at CSIS, so I didn't have any better way to approach it than to simply click and submit my CV through the Government of Canada jobs portal. No recruitment by a connected professor in a posh graduate school. I wasn't talent spotted in my business career. That would have been awesome, but no. No one was looking for me. I had to go looking for them.

The requirements to qualify to submit an application are pretty straightforward: Canadian citizenship, a degree of some sort and a valid and permanent Canadian driver's licence. The complete process for applying, however, was much more involved, with a number of stages. After submitting an application online, I had a phone interview, a group information session, psychological tests, a "suitability" interview with role playing, a larger panel interview with more role playing, a security clearance interview, a French language aptitude test, background security checks, a polygraph test and then a final executive interview.

I do remember that for most stages there was a real lack of feedback. I was left wondering each time if I had progressed or not. I would call my designated recruiter and ask for any additional information or feedback she could share. She was a friendly and responsive information black hole. I was up against a seasoned CSIS human resource professional, and she easily swatted away my best efforts to coax some intel out of her about how I was doing in the process. She would tell me calmly and repeatedly that not hearing from them was a good sign. If I did hear from them, it would be to inform me that I was no longer being considered. If I didn't hear from them, it meant that I was. I was hoping I could get some idea of when the next stages would be so I could have a sense of how long the whole process would take. She did not have any interest in providing clarifying information. I did not want to annoy her. In my mind everything was a test, so I sat and waited by the phone.

The first in-person stage in the process was the group information session. I was living in Toronto and was invited to the attend the presentation at the regional office. Without giving too much away, I can say that it's downtown.

My session would be held in a large assembly room on the same reception floor, but outside of CSIS's secure and restricted area.

It was largely an orientation about what was to come and the many stages we should expect to go through. I remember looking around that room and even at that early point in the process feeling a spirit of exclusivity and exceptionalism. It was led by our presenter, the head of recruitment. He was probably in his late thirties, with a full head of shaggy brown hair loosely parted on one side. He wore a dark grey, slightly ill-fitting suit that I'd learn was a bit of a uniform at CSIS. The role was spy, but the dress code was mid-level public service employee.

He made a point to remind us of the thousands of people who apply every year and the reality that of the thirty or forty people who were in that room, only one or maybe two would make it all the way to the end. My competitive side couldn't help but get caught up. The CSIS hiring process is not fun, but it was a gauntlet I was determined to run. It was an exclusive club and I wanted to make it in. The reality is that when you join CSIS, you realize it's a lot like any organization with a strong HR department. There are many wonderful and talented people; there are also some folks you look at and wonder, How did *you* get in here? And that of course would make you realize, Maybe I'm not so special after all?

The other important note he stressed was that we were interviewing with the Canadian Security Intelligence Service, not the Canadian Security *and* Intelligence Service. We were told if we got this wrong in our interviews, we would automatically fail. Looking back, I wonder if this was actual policy or the presenter freelancing on a personal point of annoyance. At the time it didn't matter. I wasn't going to make that mistake.

The suitability interview was the first big individual test I faced. It would be with my steel-trap HR rep and a more genial intelligence officer (what we call an IO) in the Toronto regional office. Unlike the information session, this would be held *inside* the restricted area. It was my first literal small step into CSIS—and it was almost my last.

I had prepared *a lot* for this interview. As I mentioned, prior to my UK revelation that I wanted to fight terrorism, I didn't know a lot about CSIS. We were instructed in the information interview that we would be quizzed on the CSIS Act, so I read the Act cover to cover. I made flash cards about every chapter. I wasn't a lawyer, so I found the whole thing a bit dry, but I did it. I covered warrant powers, cooperating with foreign governments, security screening responsibilities, everything. I ended up with a huge stack of flash cards covering all the minutiae of the Act. In my mind this was a test of information collection and retention. I was determined not to miss anything. I think I even had some cards with French translations.

I got so caught up in memorizing every little thing, I couldn't see the forest for the trees, and my overpreparation ended up being to my detriment, almost devastatingly so. The first question my HR rep asked me was, "What are the threats that CSIS is mandated to investigate?" This was an easy question. I mean, if you're interviewing with any organization, you should probably know what it is you will be expected to do. The threats are the core of the CSIS mandate. It is the fundamental purpose of the organization. Its raison d'être. And I drew a complete blank.

I sat there for a second in silence. I saw a look of concern cross my HR interviewer's face. It was the first trace of genuine emotion I had seen or heard her express, and it made things so much worse. I looked at my cue cards stacked in front of me. What were the odds that the card with threats to the security of Canada was on top? It wasn't. My heart sank. I started to think about how nice it was to have made it this far, slowly considering that my dream of being a spy was about to die with question number one of my very first interview. I thought about what I would do next with my life.

Mercifully the intelligence officer, my future co-worker and in that moment best friend in the world, decided to take pity on me. Whether it was because she could feel my anxiety and was trying to save herself from the growing awkward tension or because she felt some sympathy as she knew what it was like to sit in my chair, it didn't really matter. She threw me a lifeline.

"Terrorism...?" she softly hinted, her voice rising at the end of the word as if she were asking me the question.

"*Yes!* Terrorism!" I exclaimed. "Of course, terrorism!"

My blood started to circulate again, and the terrorism flash card popped back into my mind. "Terrorism, espionage and sabotage, foreign-influenced activities and subversion!"

I wanted to give her a high-five. Like we were a team. I was back in the game!

Amazingly they let me continue to the next phase of that interview, and the biggest hurdle in the whole process, the role-playing exercise. I'd be playing out a scenario with the intelligence officer. I was handed a piece of paper with the instructions and given a few minutes to quietly prepare. I was told they would start whenever I was ready and not to break character until the end of the exercise.

I'd known this part was coming, but there really isn't a way to prepare for a role-playing exercise when you aren't given the scenario in advance. All I knew was that I was not going to say Canadian Security *and* Intelligence Service. That's all I had practised. I'd learned my lesson from the earlier interview: get the basics right. "Hello, my name is Andrew, and I'm here from the Canadian Security Intelligence Service." I nailed it!

It was so silly, but once I got that out, I really relaxed. I think the other thing that helped was not having expectations about what I was supposed to achieve. Build rapport and trust, listen and gather information, ask clarifying questions, and make sure to leave the door open for future conversations, because there will inevitably be things that you wish you'd asked in the interview and you are going to want to follow up on. That was my "strategy" for my suitability interview role-playing exercise, and it didn't change much throughout my career.

I was cruising right along when suddenly the fire alarm rang out in the entire building. My first thought was, Don't break character. My second thought was, Gosh, this sure is an elaborate way to get me to break character, setting off the fire alarm in the whole building. Though it became clear pretty quickly that it wasn't. I looked at my counterpart and she looked mildly annoyed. I guess she was in a role-playing groove too and didn't want to be disrupted. In character, I turned to her and said, "I realize we may need to depart shortly; however, I would like to continue our conversation. Would you mind if I contacted you again?" She gave the game away when she paused briefly, looked out the door to see what other people were doing and then came back to sit down. "Nah, I think we'll be okay, let's keep going." The alarm stopped and we continued. The fire alarm wasn't a test, but I passed anyway.

After nearly disqualifying myself on the very first question of the recruitment process, I started to hit my stride. The next big obstacle was the National Assessment Panel (NAP). This was a panel interview including the head of recruitment, the head of HR and a couple of senior managers. I was once again in the Toronto regional office, but now I was on a higher floor and farther down the hall in an executive boardroom. With each successful stage I was making my way deeper into the office, and now I would be facing even more daunting opposition. I was seated at one end of the table with the head of recruitment, who had done the information interview group presentation, at the other. While he had a youthful appearance, the executives seated on either side of me looked more seasoned, hardened and even a little sour at being forced to participate. They gave the impression that this activity was ruining their day and they were holding it against me that they had to be there. It was certainly intimidating, but it actually could have been a worse arrangement. I could have been seated on one side and had five people across from me. This was only slightly less hostile a configuration than that. It nevertheless left me alone feeling surrounded rather than in front of a firing squad.

They peppered me with tough questions that I wasn't provided with in advance. I tried to talk through my thought process. I explained my answer and rationalization. If I got it "wrong" I was hoping for part marks for consideration and thoughtfulness. In most interviews or even conversations I typically look to the other individual for feedback or cues to see if I am on the right track or if they agree with me or not: a subtle confused tilt of the head, a nod, a smirk, leaning forward, leaning back. In this interview I didn't get much. I wouldn't say they were intentionally trying to rattle me but they certainly weren't revealing anything, which in itself was unnerving and definitely not comforting. I think some of them took pleasure in seeing someone in the hot seat and putting me through my paces.

I did my best to keep calm and answer their questions seriously, but I also started to let myself have fun with it. I even got a laugh. It was a question about what I would do in a particularly confrontational theoretical situation with a human source (this is what CSIS calls informants, as they are people who regularly provide information to our officers). Basically, it was someone I was expected to have a close existing relationship with, but in that moment we were having a difficult conversation. I ended my answer with, "I would then say to him, 'Let's hug it out ...'" It was a reference to a recent (at the time) episode of a TV show, either *The Office* or *Entourage*. The full quote is, "Let's hug it out, bitch." Now I don't think I said the full quote, but I think the head of recruitment thought I had, and despite his best attempts to hold it in, I did see him chuckle a bit to himself. I considered it a small victory and a demonstration of how I could be cool under pressure. I quickly put a lie to that notion.

They had given me a glass of water at the start of the session. After our little bonding giggle over my clever pop culture reference, I thought I might like to have a quick sip. I had done my best to give an air of confidence throughout the interview. I don't think my voice had cracked or crumbled, my feet were flat on the floor and I thought my responses were reasonably thoughtful and concise. But when I went to raise the glass of water and bring it to my lips, my hand and arm started shaking fiercely. It was like all of my anxiety and nerves just started shooting down my arm, causing my hand to tremble and the glass of water to shake. I felt it immediately and looked down at my hand to see if I could pull myself together. The glass was about two or three inches off the table. It was now shaking violently. That's as far as it ever went.

It hung there long enough that I'm sure everyone saw it. I put the glass down as gently as I could; it was like landing a plane in turbulence. I watched it intently the whole way down—I had zero confidence in my ability to land that glass of water. I got it down without any spilling, which at that point I considered a success. I pulled my hands back together on the table in front of me and just continued on as if nothing had happened. I never mentioned it, and neither did they.

I didn't hear from them for weeks this time, maybe even a couple of months. I remembered that no news was good news, but I was definitely getting a little impatient. I had taken a job as a consultant and was living with my younger brother and his girlfriend in an apartment we rented on the ground floor of a Midtown Toronto townhouse. My job and living situation were fine, but in my mind, they were both placeholders. On the one hand, I knew that the recruitment process could take a long time, so I couldn't just sit around and wait. On the other hand, if I were offered the job, I would have to move to Ottawa for the intelligence officer training course. It didn't make sense to find a permanent place of my own in Toronto or a better job until I knew if I was going to make it or not.

Finally, I got a call. I'd passed the NAP. It was time for a security interview and a deep dive into my past.

Jaywalking and Other Dark Secrets from My Past

Up to that point, as much as I was preparing for every stage and advancing through the recruitment process, in the back of my mind I don't know if I ever really thought it would happen. I knew the stats. Thousands of people apply. Some years only a few dozen make it. The odds were always bad, and by no means did I ever feel confident that the one to make it would be me. I was enjoying the process, though. I was certainly trying my best, but ultimately it felt very outside the realm of possibility that I would actually be offered the job.

I had so little confidence that I hadn't told anyone I was even applying. Not my mother, my three brothers or my new girlfriend of a few months. I just assumed at one point I'd get a letter in the mail that said, "Thanks but no thanks," and that would be that. Why tell everyone if it wasn't going to work out anyway? In my thinking, years later I would have a rejection letter as a souvenir to prove that at one point I'd applied. It would be a keepsake from the experience. With each phone call I got closer to making it, but it still didn't feel real until the next paperwork I received. It wasn't a letter; it was a form.

The security clearance and background check application required the names, birth dates and hometowns of everyone in my family, as well as non-related character references who would be interviewed to speak on my behalf. Now it was no longer just some fun thing that I could keep secret. Shit was getting real. I was going to have to have some awkward conversations with some of the people closest to me.

So as we were sitting around the table of an extended Sunday night family dinner I announced to everyone that I was in the process of applying to CSIS. I told them that I'd started to apply months ago, and I had advanced to a significant enough stage that I thought it was a real possibility I could make it.

In the vetting process CSIS was conducting on me, my family would now be checked out too—whether they liked it or not. I wanted to give them an opportunity to say whether they were in the "or not" category. I think I phrased it very matter-of-factly: "I am applying for top secret security clearance and I need to give the government all of your information. If there is any reason why you would like me *not* to do that, please speak now or forever hold your peace."

Fortunately, there were no confessions that night. A little confusion and lots of questions about what CSIS was and where I was in the process, but that was it. Everyone was supportive. Truth be told, we probably should have had a more open discussion. As much as this was my decision, their lives would be affected too. When I became a spy, I would ask them to lie to everyone they knew about where I worked and what I was doing. It was more to ask than I knew at the time. At that family dinner, though, that reality still seemed very far away.

CSIS didn't interview any of my family but they did check my references. I had given them a list of people who had known me most of my life. One was a childhood friend who had just started his career as a junior researcher at a financial services firm in Toronto. I had told him CSIS would be reaching out for a security clearance application I had submitted related to my army reserve career, which was already well under way, so he wasn't totally surprised when they asked to meet. I do think his employer was, though. The CSIS security screeners showed up at his office and announced their presence at reception. As he told me later, their receptionist came to the open-plan office where all the analysts sat together and announced quite loudly, "Mike [not his real name], CSIS is here to see you." He said it was a like a scene in a movie where the whole office suddenly got quiet and everyone turned their chairs to get a look at this new guy. One senior analyst blurted out loudly, "Who the fuck did we just hire?" I'm not sure if he ever lived that down, and I can't believe he didn't totally tank my reference check as payback.

The security checks ran in the background as my own process continued. Each stage was a stressful and unique experience; probably none more of both and none more distinct to CSIS than the polygraph test. There just aren't many other jobs that require it. To make matters worse, I'm what you would call a pleaser. I want people to like me. I want to be helpful to others, and it stresses me out when someone else is upset or uncomfortable. If a situation gets tense, I'm the first person to tell a joke to try to lighten the mood. It's a great reflex at dinner parties but not so helpful during a polygraph test.

They used a small vacant room in the Toronto regional office. It was the size of a large walk-in closet. It was furnished but lacked any personal charm that might have been a distraction for the test. I sat down in a chair and got hooked up to the machine.

For all the issues I have with movie depictions of spies, I have to admit they actually get the polygraph pretty accurate. Just call me Greg Focker from *Meet the Parents*. My polygraphist was definitely straight out of central casting. He was in his late fifties, a little dishevelled in a slightly oversized brown blazer, with a permanent scowl that would force him to only play the bad cop in any interrogation scene. He asked me if I was comfortable. I considered making a joke about "the circle of trust" but thought better of it.

I can't remember the exact wording of the first question, but what I heard was, "Have you ever done anything bad in your entire life?" And this is when the pleaser in me kicked in: Where do I start!

I've lived a pretty upright existence—there are definitely things I wish I had done differently or better, but nothing that I'm overly ashamed of. That said, everything I've ever done wrong I feel absolutely terrible about. I started the confessional, "One time when I was ten or eleven years old, I was with a group of kids and we ripped off the hood ornament of a Mercedes-Benz for no particular reason. I felt sick about it at the time and still feel bad today."

I could see the polygraphist take a deep breath. "Any more recent examples?" He only wanted to hear about things he thought were relevant and clearly didn't want to be there all day. I wanted to make sure I didn't leave anything out. It wasn't a good mix.

Next I told him about how I'd plagiarized sections of a grade seven book report for French class, and how I felt bad about not calling some girls back after first dates. The polygraphist seemed frustrated, which only made me more anxious. To calm down I tried to remind myself what I thought CSIS was looking for. Can I be blackmailed for something I've done that would make me compromise my loyalty to Canada? I'm certainly embarrassed about many things in my life, but nothing I'm so ashamed of that I would give up secrets to keep from being exposed.

I couldn't see most of what I was hooked up to. I assumed from the movies that somewhere in the room there was a needle moving over a piece of paper, measuring my responses. I imagined my needle slowing down as more questions came and the reflection on the boringness of my life washed over me.

Just as I started to feel a little better, the polygraphist said to me, "What about criminality?" Then he added, "I mean, we get guys in the chair and we think everything is fine and then we find out they have illegally downloaded music from the internet." Oh no! The needle started flying around again.

This predates streaming; in the early days there were sites like Napster and LimeWire where you could download movies and music for free. I certainly did do that. I said, "Downloading music is illegal, isn't it?"

"Of course it is," he said.

"Well I've done that," I sheepishly admitted.

"Well, a few songs shouldn't be too bad," he turned the knife.

"I've got thousands!" I replied, concerned.

My mind was racing to anything else that I hadn't realized was illegal. I felt like my needle might break off the machine. Jaywalking and times when I hadn't paid for parking were all that came to mind.

I wanted to be honest because I didn't want it to look like I was hiding anything, but I couldn't remember anything. I could tell my polygraphist wasn't satisfied with my answers, which was only adding to my stress. If he wanted to rattle me, mission accomplished.

I never got to see the results of my polygraph, but I guess I passed. I got the job. And I never downloaded anything illegal ever again knowing I would be having that fun again in another five years, when my refresh was due. Something to look forward to.

The Inner Sanctum

I started my recruitment milling about the ground-floor lobby of the CSIS office building in Toronto. By the time I made it to the final stage, the executive interview, I was at the highest and innermost office of the building. I believe at this point it was a foregone conclusion I was going to be hired. It certainly felt that way. It was much more collegial than the previous stages. The interviewer was the person in charge of the Toronto regional office. He would go on to rise to director of operations (second in command) for the entire organization. He could not have been nicer. It was like a boss getting to know a new employee. Tell me about yourself: Do you have a family? What would you like to get out of your CSIS career?

He made it a point to stress and return again to the issue of mobility. I was given this speech at every stage, by everyone I spoke to at CSIS in the hiring process. The Service reserves the right to move you where they need you. The wrinkle at this moment was the pending reality of it all. If I were hired, I would move to Ottawa for training. There was no knowing how long it would take me to get back to Toronto.

It was a positive conversation. He didn't ask me any hard questions and I didn't give him any reason to. I was excited to be there, and I don't think I hid it well. I was eager, earnest, excited and deferential. I almost couldn't believe it. This crazy idea I'd had of becoming a spy felt very real. This was the final stage of a fifteen-month battle of attrition, and for the first time I allowed myself to believe that I had won.

I honestly can't remember if I got an email or received a welcome package in the mail. I do remember speaking with my recruiter on the phone and her asking me when I could start. I think it was August and she had a French language class spot ready for me in September. After the cold shoulder I'd got in response to every inquiry, I desperately wanted to say in that moment, "You take fifteen months to move me through this process and then ask me to move my life in a couple weeks?" Of course, what I said was, "Absolutely, whatever you need."

I told my family. They were excited. Their next question was, What do they tell people? I didn't have any more information yet. I said, "Don't tell anyone anything. Say that I'm moving to Ottawa to work for the government doing policy work." That was my degree from university, so it made sense. I told them, "I'll let you know more as soon as I do." I was positive there would be more instructions now that I was officially an employee. (Spoiler alert: There weren't.)

My girlfriend and I had a more involved conversation. We had only been together for about six months at that point. It would have been easy to call it quits. Ottawa was a long way away, and I don't think either of us was particularly excited about a long-distance relationship. Ottawa wasn't a permanent post, though. There was a chance I could get back. I had to complete French training and then intelligence officer training. That would be about a year and a half. After that I could get a posting in the Toronto office. There was a light at the end of the tunnel. Everyone stressed throughout the recruitment process that mobility was tricky and just because you wanted Toronto didn't mean you would get it. On the flip side, Toronto was the largest regional office, so there were better than zero odds. It was a gamble, and we rolled the dice that it would all work out. (Another spoiler alert: It didn't.)

3

SPY UNIVERSITY

T HINGS REALLY started to move at that point. What had been a very long and deliberate hiring process became an expedited relocation. I drove down to Ottawa with my girlfriend and bought a small condo near CSIS's headquarters over a weekend. It wasn't an expensive place and I furnished it appropriately with entire rooms copied almost directly from the IKEA catalogue. The government paid for movers to collect what few possessions I had at my brother's place, but there really wasn't much. Not many things had come back with me from London and I hadn't acquired much in Toronto, knowing that this move might come.

Having been hired, I had a tremendous feeling of accomplishment. It was a goal realized and I was excited about the real adventure ahead of me. I was moving to a new city, living on my own for the first time in my life (I had always had roommates to that point). I didn't know anyone well in Ottawa and I had no idea what my actual job would involve. I couldn't wait to find out. But before I could, I had one last requirement for the government I had to satisfy. Before they would teach me how to be a spy, I had to learn French.

This was not a surprise. I'd known about the French requirement for the job and I'd worried quite a bit about it. Despite being a decent overall student, I was terrible at languages. I had struggled through the mandated French classes from elementary school to grade ten, at which point I'd decided I'd drop French and take Spanish instead. When would I ever need French? I thought at the time. I'll cut my losses and start fresh with a new language. What a mistake. I probably remembered one word of French for every year I'd studied it.

Fast-forward to the fall of 2007 and the nine months I would spend in Ottawa's French language training. I won't dwell on this phase of my journey because there is no need for you to suffer hearing about it, after all I experienced suffering through it. I respect the French language and I appreciate that government employees in certain roles need to be able to communicate with their employees and the public in both official languages. And again, I knew that it was a requirement of the job.

That said, the government-sponsored French language class in Ottawa was a soul-destroying, laborious and ineffective exercise in passing a test. There were four of us in the class. Every morning we would sit around the table and say, "Qu'est-ce que vous avez fait hier soir?" To translate, What did you do last night? We were there every day and nobody led a very exciting life. "Pas grand-chose," or not much, was the constant refrain.

In addition to my limited nightlife activities (and vocabulary), I also felt constrained by the fact that I was now officially employed to be a spy but still had no idea what I was allowed to say about what I did or why I was even in French school—especially to our well-meaning teacher, who we were led to believe did not know and should not be told of our true employment.

The exams consisted of reading, writing and oral interaction. The grading was: A, lowest score; B, intermediate; C, advanced; and E, exempt. It was the exact opposite of how I or anyone might expect A, B and C grades to be ranked compared to every system of grading I had ever experienced. Perhaps something was lost in translation. The requirement was to achieve a score of Bs at all three levels.

It reminded me of an old joke my boss at the bank had told me before my financial services exam. He said, "Andrew, a passing grade on the test is seventy percent, and a perfect score on the test is seventy percent."

Long story short, I passed. I was officially bilingual and, more importantly, I was done with French school. It was time to start my training.

Class # [REDACTED]: Freshman Orientation

The first day of my intelligence officer training class was September 2, 2008. I will remember that date forever. In fact, every IO remembers their first day of training: it is the start date for accumulating pensionable time and the pay anniversary for annual raises. The starting salary for an IO was fifty thousand dollars and it went up in pre-determined increments for the first five years of an IO's career. This was our probationary period. The increases were not regular, though. They varied between two and three percent for the first four pay raises and then somewhere around fifteen to eighteen percent in year five. It was called the five-year bump and it was a huge deal. Every IO could tell you exactly how far away they were from their bump. My clock was just starting.

Intelligence officer training classes are a lot like freshman orientation groups at university. There are people from all over the country brought together into this hodgepodge of a class at the same time for the same purpose. There were nineteen of us in one class, and there was another with eighteen running at the same time. It hasn't always been the case that there are so many people in multiple classes. I was part of a post-9/11 bubble of training. The Service had received additional funding, and they poured it into hiring more intelligence officers. Throughout my time this tap would turn on and off and back on again. My class was probably near the tail end of the post-9/11 wave.

Most of us were new to Ottawa, and like me, many hoped to return to their home cities when they were done training. This made accommodations and planning tricky. However, since transfers are so frequent, CSIS has a team of relocation specialists who offer practical and financial assistance with moves. I took advantage of some incentives when I purchased the condo in the Ottawa suburbs, knowing similar help would be available if I was to (fingers crossed) move again in a couple years. A lot of my classmates took another option, which was to be housed close together in furnished accommodations in downtown Ottawa. For them, it was almost like a dorm setting and it also helped foster the freshman year vibe. We'd work long hours together and even had special tables in the headquarters cafeteria reserved just for us. Coupling was not unusual. There were many casual hook-ups and more than a few training class marriages. I was close with my classmates, but my living arrangement and long-distance relationship meant that I wasn't a full participant in the after-school and weekend social scene.

All classes are given a number. I cannot reveal my class number as that may allow you math wizards out there to infer the number of IOs at CSIS, and that is classified. When CSIS was created in 1984, the founding members of the organization were RCMP members who transferred over to the newly established organization. They brought with them policing backgrounds, experience and culture. Class number one was the first civilian class trained specifically to be intelligence officers. There are stories of the original classes learning how to jump out of a plane and detonate bombs—which is kind of crazy considering CSIS was always intended to be a domestic intelligence service.

A lot of our day-to-day work would be research and analysis, which was done using corporate applications and databases. The CSIS systems were unique to the Service so they were new to all of us. A large part of training was learning how to navigate them to make sure we were capturing and analyzing all the relevant information we needed. The classic training example is looking up the number of variations of how people spell "Saskatchewan." There are a lot! When searching the databases, it was important to make sure we didn't miss a result because someone used the short form "Sask" or misspelled it "Saskatchawan." People could also be referred to using many different names or nicknames—think about all the variations of Mike, Michael or Mikey in Canada. Or Jackson, Jaxon, Jacks and Jax. It could be incredibly frustrating and a little terrifying to be looking for something and not find it when you think everyone else has it.

There were also dedicated communications platforms we used to send messages and share information both internally and with partners. I had a constant fear of entering the wrong delivery address and inadvertently sending classified information outside of CSIS or starting a horrible "reply all" scenario where the entire organization was reading my training report, wondering why they got it and who the idiot was that sent it. In all of those moments of uncertainty and doubt, it was a relief to have classmates who were open to sharing their answers and working collaboratively.

Training was the place where we were supposed to make mistakes, and believe me, we all made mistakes. We'd debrief in the morning and if someone had really screwed up, they'd bring donuts in for the rest of the class. If you saw donuts in the morning, you knew there'd be a good story in the morning debrief. Soon it would be my turn to go pastry shopping.

Feliz Navidad

One of my training runs provided two of the biggest lessons I would learn. One was intentional and the other just a strange fluke. We had been working our way through a source development role-playing exercise. Human sources, or confidential informants, are the lifeblood of the intelligence service. People are the eyes and ears in their communities and are most likely able to access sensitive, privileged or otherwise not readily shared information.

One quick side note: in addition to human source reporting, referred to as HUMINT, there is also open-source information (OSINT) from publicly available sources, signals intelligence (SIGINT) from intercepted technical communication, and a CSIS special, RUMINT, which was the gossip and rumours passed around the cafeteria about hidden relationships and potential job movements at work.

Back to the exercise . . . Our job as intelligence officers was to collect information. Often that involved finding people who either had or had access to threat-related information and recruiting them to work with us. In our training, they had ex-CSIS employees as role players to simulate the experience of meeting and recruiting these people. At the beginning of the course, I was handed a fake name and a phone number for my personal role player. I was told he was someone who was believed to have access to sensitive information. It would be my job to assess him, evaluate the information and try to recruit the role player to continue to work with me and become a human source. The first step was simply to phone him up and arrange a meeting. At subsequent stages we would be given various scenarios we might use to develop the relationship; for example, needing to move our conversation from a coffee shop to a hotel room to discuss a sensitive matter. It was all designed to more or less replicate the source recruitment and management process.

For this exercise, it was my contact who called me. We had met a few times at this point and had developed a good rapport. He called and said it was an emergency and he had to see me as soon as possible. He told me to meet him at a mall in Ottawa in twenty minutes. It was designed to be rushed and a little frantic, but it wasn't unfair. Ideally, I would have known the mall we were going to and had a sense of how to coordinate a safe meeting there. In this case I didn't. I was new to Ottawa and had never been to it.

I tried to get there early to look around and get the lay of the land. It was Christmastime and the mall was extremely busy. We had planned to meet in the food court. It was packed and loud, which made me slightly uncomfortable, but I thought at least the ambient noise would give us some cover for whatever extremely important matter we had to discuss.

He found me easily enough in the crowd and hurried over to join me at my small table. Before I had a chance to say hello, he said, "I have something for you," and stuffed a small package into my work bag. I tried to look down to see what it was but he forced me to concentrate on him as he leaned across the table towards me with concern and said he recognized someone at a food court table nearby. He then sat back in his chair nervously and waited for me to tell him what to do. He was a pretty good actor, and he really sold his concern. I didn't know it at the time, but he was making this up. It was a test . . . and I failed. I said, "Oh, we better move then."

Looking back, this was wrong. If he was worried about being caught together then we shouldn't have been meeting in public. If he had to meet in public, it should have been quick, and we should have had a cover story in place about who I was and why we were meeting. Instead we got up and started walking away from the table together. That's when I learned how completely wrong I was.

We made our way down to the main concourse. There was a seasonal band playing Christmas songs, entertaining the shoppers and passersby. They were just wrapping up their last song as we approached. It was a version of "Feliz Navidad," and I will remember it forever. The music had been conveniently providing some ambient noise to our conversation. It suddenly stopped and when it did, as if on cue, the lead guitarist looked out into the crowd and recognized my source. He called out loudly to him by name and walked over to the both of us to say, "*Hola.*"

Like the fire alarm during my role-playing exercise in recruitment, my first thought was, Holy shit, CSIS has gone through with an elaborate ruse of planting someone in the mall band on the off chance that the handler walks his source nearby. Then I realized the guitarist must have called my role player by his real name (it was not the name I was calling him), so it was all just a totally random coincidence. He had told me at the food court he recognized someone, but that was made up to test me. This was real, for both of us. And at that moment, neither one of us knew what to do. I didn't want to break character, but we didn't have a cover story. What was the script I was supposed to stick with? I didn't know anything about my role player so I couldn't make up a plausible story about what we were doing together.

I now looked over at him. I was officially out of my depth. He was ex-CSIS and experienced, so he should've been able to handle things. This was his real-life friend who may or may not have known where he worked. I scanned his face to get a read on how he thought we should play it out and quickly realized he was just as confused about what to do or say as I was.

In these situations, the handler (me in this scenario) is supposed to take control. We are the professionals. We do the talking or at the very least provide some direction. However, I felt like we were now outside the bounds of our exercise and I didn't want to create any issues in this role player's life by coming up with a convoluted story. So, I just kind of bailed on him. It was one step up from telling someone at a party you're going to the bathroom and leaving. I basically pretended I didn't know the guy. I said, "Thank you for the directions to the food court," and I just walked off.

I walked back up to the food court and waited a minute. I didn't know what else to do. That should have been that. Lesson learned. Don't wander around with a source and walk into an area you don't have control over. But that wasn't the only lesson . . . my night wasn't over yet.

I had to see my role player again because of what he had given me—it was an old-school CD-ROM (it was even old in training) and apparently it had some crucial information on it. The only problem was, I didn't think I was allowed to have it. As we were walking, before we were interrupted, I had asked him what it was that he had placed in my bag. He told me it was a CD. He had seen the subject of our mock investigation using a computer, and it had looked like he was reviewing the contents of this CD. He thought it had names or cities or something important on it. When the subject had left, he'd forgotten his CD and my source had scooped it up, thinking that I would be interested. Obviously I was interested, but I didn't think I was entitled to the contents. This was the *intended* lesson of the evening. Was I allowed to take that CD? Would I take it?

The following morning, we all met back at the classroom to talk about the exercise. Feliz Navidad, everyone! My turn to bring the donuts. We then had an animated discussion about whether we could take the CD. Would it matter if the CD was in the garbage when the source took it? What if the source took the CD out of a lost-and-found box rather than a desk? What were the security implications of taking the CD? What if the subject of investigation went back that night and realized it was missing? People did not agree. The consensus was we shouldn't be taking information we did not have rightful access to. That said, there were many impassioned pleas about whether people would still feel that way if there were an attack that could have been avoided with the information on that disk. After a lot of hair splitting and many creative solutions proposed by the students, the trainers still said, "No."

So, did I take the CD? A lot of these things crossed my mind in the few minutes I had to regroup sitting in the food court, waiting for my source to come back. I should say *hoping* my source would come back. Thankfully he did. We both snapped back into character without even mentioning the awkwardness of the previous situation, and ultimately, I didn't take it. I told him, "You have to put this back. I do want to know what's on it, but we'll have to find another way." He asked if I was sure but didn't put up a fight. I honestly didn't know if I was right. I thought a lot about it that night and exchanged a flurry of text messages with my classmates who had gone through the same exercise, ahead of our class debrief. Years later as an investigator I was confronted with a similar scenario. It had to do with someone's mail. It was pretty murky, and it was real life. I'll get to that one later.

Frankly Speaking

Among our database searches, role-playing exercises and report-writing practice, there were a few independent assignments and activities, one of which was actually a great indicator of just how tough the job can be and how small a world it really is. We were gathered one afternoon after class. On our itinerary it just said, "Reserved all evening." We didn't know what we would be doing. We got to the classroom and were handed our assignments: we were to go out into Ottawa and find someone to talk to. We were each given a separate location (to ensure we didn't all end up at the same place) and told to find a stranger and engage that person in conversation to see what we could find out. We were not given specific instructions on what information we were looking for; we were just told to see what we could get. These would not be role players. This was real life. It wasn't meant to be an intrusive experience for our unknowing targets; we were just supposed to see if we could make a new friend. Cold, on the spot.

I entered my designated location, a small Irish pub, around 7 p.m. Our class had been scattered to pubs, bars and restaurants throughout downtown Ottawa. We were told to report back to another bar around 10 p.m. All of our trainers and fellow classmates would be at the rallying pub and we would have an opportunity to debrief and share our experience. So I had three hours, which wasn't a long time but certainly was long enough to find someone to talk to. I surveyed the bar. It was pretty empty. I didn't have a lot of options.

In my mind the ideal situation was that there would be sports on TV and there would be some guys sitting around watching. I didn't even care what sport. I had confidence I could fake my way through most, even a soccer conversation. Having lived in London, I had extensive knowledge of the English Premier League (as long as it was between 2002 and 2005). It was not to be.

The TV was showing the news. There was a woman sitting alone at the bar, though. It looked like she had just arrived and was order-ing dinner. She was late forties/early fifties with long greying brown hair. She was casually dressed in jeans and a loose sweatshirt. There were a few young couples having dinner with friends in booths. Although they were closer to my age, I could not think of a scenario where I could join a table of four friends eating dinner and slip into the conversation seamlessly. Certainly not in a pub where it was oth-erwise quiet and there were a lot of empty tables. The lady alone at the bar was my best chance, and unless I went elsewhere, she was my only chance.

I sat down beside her. I asked the bartender for a menu and a beer. I went with a classic, "How's it going?"

"Fine," she responded. She was eating dinner alone at a bar on a weeknight, so I went out on a limb.

"You in from out of town?" She was. Success!

"Me too," I responded. "What brings you by?"

She worked for the federal government. She was in town visiting their head office for a few days. She asked me the same question, and I told her I was working in finance and from Toronto. I was in town for some meetings.

There weren't a lot of rules or restrictions on the exercise. Walk-ing into that pub, in my mind the goal of the exercise was for me to feel comfortable approaching a stranger and talking to them without giving too much of myself away. Did I have the nerve to sidle up to a random person at the bar and make a new friend? Just as important, I thought, was whether I could keep my story straight. Why was I there? Where was I staying? What questions would I get asked that I needed to have answers to? This person wasn't a role player. She was just a woman getting a bite to eat and now she was an unknowing participant in my undercover training. Could I lie to her convincingly? For some that might not seem like a big deal. This was my first real-world test to see if I could stomach it.

My food arrived and we continued our small talk. She liked working for the government. She had two kids who were around my age. One kid seemed like they were okay, but it was clear the other one was struggling. Rather than give a superficial answer, she opened up in a way that made me feel like she was happy to get some things off her chest. It sounded like a mixture of drugs and mental health challenges. In that part of the conversation, I felt slightly uncomfortable with the circumstances that had brought me there.

It was an unsolicited admission. I hadn't been pressing for personal information, I was just trying to engage her in conversation. In that moment, though, I felt like I did achieve another goal of the exercise. Her candour might have been because it was easier for her to talk to a stranger, but I also felt like I did a good job in making her feel comfortable enough to share something so private.

I would actually encourage anyone who wants to be a spy to try this activity. It may sound simple enough. But try it and see. If you find it easy in practice, then that is a good indication that you could be a field investigator. If you are uneasy with it all, if you find it awkward to strike up a conversation with someone on a random weeknight, tough to get them to open up to you, and if it doesn't sit right when they do, well, you aren't alone.

This was my first taste of really lying on the job to a stranger. It's harmless, I told myself at the time. It didn't feel great, but I did it and cleared a small personal hurdle on my path to being an IO.

In another pub that same night one of my classmates became a legend. He walked into his assigned location and was presented with an even worse scenario than I had. The only patrons in his establishment were a small group of people sitting together having a social drink. He somehow managed to join them, and as he was meeting everyone, he couldn't help but notice it was a very eclectic group.

They were all from the United States, but many different ethnic and geographic backgrounds. They had language skills and seemed highly educated in a variety of fields. To him, it felt like a very odd mix of people to be out having a drink together.

He assumed he was jumping to conclusions because of his own professional circumstance. Of course, his suspicions were confirmed the next morning as he walked into the office: in the lobby of the CSIS headquarters, there sat his drinking buddies from the night before. They were from a US agency, in town to meet with their CSIS counterparts.

My classmate gave them a smile as he walked by but didn't stop to chat. He went right to the trainer's office to explain the situation. I can only imagine what was running through our American friends' heads when they saw the random guy they had been openly socializing with the night before walk past them into the CSIS office. They wouldn't take kindly to seemingly having their visiting delegation spied on.

The incident was reported up to the highest levels. Ultimately a very senior individual from CSIS made a call over to the local attaché from the US agency. Thankfully the Americans did have a sense of humour about the whole thing and there were no hard feelings. They even got my classmate a small gift—I think it was either an engraved pen or a challenge coin, the type of gift you give a visiting dignitary or someone who gives a guest lecture or presentation. Nevertheless, we thought it was awesome. We were still trainees and one of our own had "infiltrated" the Americans. It was the real deal, against people who should have been trained to detect and avoid that kind of approach. He even had a "trophy" from them as a token of respect. We all revelled in his accomplishment.

The Manila Envelope of Relationship Death

Throughout my training I was still with my Toronto girlfriend. I was commuting regularly back and forth on weekends and she would come and visit me in Ottawa. In some ways long distance was easier. I was free to work late and not have to explain where I was and what I was doing. I could give vague updates over the phone, and that seemed to be enough to tell her about my training.

In fact, in some ways it was tougher when she did come out with my classmates to socialize. There were things we couldn't talk about openly, inside jokes that didn't make any sense to anyone but us. It was this amazingly intense and secret experience that the nineteen of us were going through, and it would have been impossible to fully explain it—even if we were allowed to talk openly about it, which we weren't.

I was sensitive enough to make sure my girlfriend felt included, but I'm sure she could feel some of the hesitation in the conversations. The intentional gaps in the details. The winks and nudges to imply the things we weren't allowed to discuss. We weren't the only couple who struggled.

The reason we kept going was because there was a light at the end of the mobility tunnel. My IO course was winding down and there was a possibility I would get back to Toronto again. Near the end of training we were asked to select our placement preferences. I put the Toronto regional office as my number one choice. I figured we would be told where we were heading in January—we were scheduled to graduate at the end of that month and report to our new desks in February. I was surprised, therefore, when we all arrived in class one day in mid-December to find personally addressed, nondescript manila envelopes on our desks. They were labelled and placed in front of our assigned seats.

For my generation, it was like receiving university acceptance letters in the mail. We knew exactly what they were. Some of us opened them right away in the classroom, while others took them away to more private spaces in the building. The contents of these envelopes would dictate where we would start our careers. For some of my classmates it was an early Christmas present. Mine was a lump of coal. I didn't get Toronto. I got my second choice. Numbers two through six didn't matter for me—they were *all* desks in Ottawa. I was staying put. As a first job placement, it would be a minimum of two years.

That was a long time.

I had moved to Ottawa committed to my new career but with the hope that I would be able to quickly return to Toronto and maintain my existing relationship. In my mind the strain would just be the geography. What I didn't anticipate was how training would really be the start of a totally separate life. There were things I would never be able to share with anyone outside of that world.

Being in the same city might have helped, but the intensity of the pull into my new reality and the increasing number of secrets it left between us ultimately created far more distance in the relationship than the four-hour car ride. We broke up in late January before I even started my new placement at headquarters.

O Canada

The culmination of IO training is the "graduation." The ceremony would take place in a small auditorium in the CSIS headquarters, which was a modest but nice space for a nondescript government building built in the nineties. A small reception with coffee and muffins would be held in an adjacent seldom-used lounge. The director was scheduled to make a short speech to the attendees. Each graduate would come forward to receive their badge, a leather-bound copy of the CSIS mandate and a certificate for completing training, and to pose for a photo. Later there would be a class photo and a speech by a representative from each class.

I believe it was in the middle of the week at 10 a.m. Everyone was allowed two guests and the names needed to be submitted in advance. It was pretty inconvenient and neither my girlfriend nor my mother could make it. I didn't push them or ask anyone else if they wanted to come. We were spies, I thought, so I'd just keep it low key. A lot of other families did come. People flew in from all over the country. Classmates begged for one or two more spots. For them it was a big deal; it didn't hit me just how much it would mean to me until it began.

Before this short ceremony began, the screen for the projector came down and everyone was asked to rise for the national anthem.

We all stood, and an incredibly sappy video accompanying the anthem began. There were geese flying over lakes, ice-covered mountains, soldiers hugging children, flags waving. You could not make a more Canadian video if you were trying.

I was on my own, so I started to look around the room for a classmate I could make a face at—trying to find acknowledgement or validation on how sappy and silly I thought the production was. Instead I saw guests who were bawling. They were just totally overcome with patriotism and pride. And that was before the actual formal ceremony. It only got more emotional from there as one by one we were paraded before the CSIS director to receive our swag and have our photo taken. There were no other cameras allowed either, so everyone was totally in the moment, taking it all in. Myself now included.

I think back on that ceremony a lot. I remember the tears and the pride. My classmates' families, who had come from coast to coast and from many different ethnic backgrounds, were totally overcome because their child, spouse, brother, sister had chosen to sign up to protect and defend this country. It just meant so much to them. I know I can be cynical, and the job has a way of beating you down a bit. The emotional display triggered by the video and graduation processional was a very meaningful demonstration of appreciation for our commitment and service. It was also a display of love for Canada itself, the place I was now duty bound to protect. In that moment I was so proud of what I was doing, I would have run through a wall for my country. All these years later, and retired from the Service, it still makes me feel good about having been a part of it all.

4

ANALYST LIFE

W HEN SOMEONE thinks of spies, they probably think of John le Carré novels, James Bond, or one of my favourites, Melissa McCarthy in the movie *Spy* (when she gets out from behind her desk). What all these examples have in common is they depict what we would call field agents, or investigators. In Canada, our intelligence officers are expected to play two roles. First is this romanticized classic investigator role, knocking on doors, recruiting sources and generally collecting information.

The other role is what we call "analyst." I'm sure there is a definition of intelligence analyst somewhere. The intelligence officer analyst position at CSIS, however, is basically a catch-all title that can include any of the operational support functions that are involved in investigations but aren't in the field. It's the desk work that largely takes place sitting in front of a computer reading reports, processing information and then writing more reports. Regular headquarters analyst duties may also include complaining about lack of parking at headquarters, butting heads with field investigators in the region and coming up with any number of reasons to hold a meeting with anyone outside the building.

There are analyst positions in regional offices such as Toronto. However, in my time, the majority of IO analyst work was done at

Ottawa HQ, and when you were in a regional office you were a field investigator. As IOs we were expected to be able to do both. Mobility meant they could place you anywhere geographically and also move you between these two distinct roles.

SOS from HSP

My first posting out of training was in an analyst support role in the human source operational support (HSOS) department, in what I'll call the human source policy (HSP) section of HSOS. It was the policy control centre for human source operations across the Service. Without getting too much into specifics, not everyone who CSIS talks to is considered a human source. And there are rules and guidelines about who we could meet and what we could ask people to do, with lots of checks and balances—from casually meeting someone all the way up to formally recruiting and managing (what we would call "handling") human sources.

I was responsible for making sure these policies were being adhered to by CSIS intelligence officers and the human sources themselves. Managing human sources required ongoing documentation, justification and approvals. It was my job to review the files and make assessments on the relative merits of the recruitment, the sources and the level of sign-off needed on the various stages of the operations. The source handlers would send me a message about what they needed or wanted. I would review the reports and draft briefing notes to senior managers explaining the circumstances and what they were required to authorize, and why.

It was as much of a desk job as you could possibly give an intelligence officer at CSIS. I was stationed in a windowless office I shared with two other HSP analysts. Our computers all faced opposite walls. The room was painted institutional white. There was no art. We didn't even have a plant. We lived as though getting comfortable was a signal that we were happy to settle in. We sometimes joked about getting a poster of a window. We never did. We all wanted to get out as fast as we could, so office greenery was an investment we weren't willing to make.

More broadly, CSIS headquarters is about as bureaucratic an office environment as it gets. It's got a real nine-to-five public servant vibe. Well, actually it's whatever your core hours are. Some of my co-workers preferred 7:30 to 3:30. I was more of an 8:30-to-4:30 man. We actually had to designate someone each week to stick around until 5 p.m. We unironically called it the "late shift."

Each HSP analyst supported different regional offices. Every morning I'd sit at my computer to see if any messages had come into my inbox overnight. If they had, I read them and responded appropriately. Sometimes there weren't any, so I'd just have to sit and wait until they arrived, filling my time reviewing files or scrolling the intranet for entertainment. CSIS has an intranet for employee communication with a buy-and-sell section—a low-rent Kijiji for spies—that was a constant source of amusement. It's mostly for people who are relocating and looking to get out of car leases or rent out their homes and apartments. There was always some unintentional comedy gold: an adult prince costume (not at Halloween); one woman who constantly posted that she was selling boxes of old romance novels; someone desperately looking for a wooden owl to scare off aggressive woodpeckers; a never-worn prom dress (so sad).

If anyone called me, it was usually because there was an issue. Nobody ever called the policy shop to say thank you or to tell me how well they were adhering to policy. I had a standing joke when the phone would ring. If someone started the conversation by asking how I was doing, I liked to respond with the same question: "You tell me how I'm doing. Is my day about to get messed up? How long is the memo I'm about to write?"

It was in jest, but it was true. My days were spent responding to and solving other people's administrative issues. It wasn't at all what I'd thought I was getting myself into when I'd decided to submit my application to CSIS almost two years before. I wasn't even a cool analyst like you'd see in movies, tracking down the courier to try to find Osama bin Laden, banging on my desk that I saw something nobody else saw. Nope, I was a policy compliance officer.

I have to admit it was a tough time for me. It was humbling. I joined CSIS to fight terrorism and save the world. Now here I was almost two years into my chosen career, and I was reading about other agents' operational exploits, and my contribution was to make sure they had cited the correct policy in their reports. What's worse, I couldn't talk to anyone about how frustrating it all was. I couldn't tell my friends or family what I was doing or why I was down about it. Looking back, I'm not sure why. I mean, what would have been the harm of telling my family I was doing policy work for CSIS when I wanted to be in the field? We were always told to be discreet, and for whatever reason I kept thinking that if my cover was blown, I wouldn't be able to participate in some hypothetical deep-cover clandestine operation. I'm not exactly sure what I thought I might be needed for, given I was a white, Jewish kid from Toronto with zero language skills beyond my level-B French.

I can tell you, though, the cliché of conflict or jealousy between the headquarters analysts and the field agents is an exaggeration of an underlying truth. At least for me, from behind my desk, there was some envy and even awe of those who were on the front lines. I remember sitting in an office shooting the shit with a couple of my analyst colleagues and a manager who had just come back after a few years as an investigator in the Toronto regional office. We were talking about our future plans and what had brought him back to Ottawa. He basically said, "It gets old. Checking in and out of hotels, knocking on doors, it just gets old after a while."

It stuck out because of how crazy it sounded to me at the time. I was writing briefing notes and memos of operational files I wasn't even a part of. I dreamed every day of meeting a source in a hotel room. It felt so close and so far away, and this guy was giving it all up?

I was incredulous, and I wasn't alone. I looked quickly at my analyst friends. They couldn't believe what they were hearing either.

Maverick, Iron Man and Ron Burgundy Walk into a Hotel...

The best part of my job, by far, was choosing code names. I don't think it's a surprise to learn that CSIS uses code names for things. In fact, I imagine people expect it. Naming human sources was one of my responsibilities, and I just want to confirm it's just as much fun as you might think it would be.

Now, I didn't have a straight list of everyone's names or photos of every source working for CSIS. In fact, there are very strict rules on who knows the names of human sources. Information is extremely limited in terms of where it is stored and how it is accessed. You can't just stumble across a real name or list of code names. If you are working with CSIS as a source, I may have named you, but let me reassure you: I did file reviews and managed source administration for some people for years, and I still wouldn't know it if I walked by them on the street.

There are a number of rules for choosing a code name. The most basic was to be wary of offensive or even overly goofy names. Part of my job was writing memos to senior leadership if there were problems on a source file. I didn't want to have to inform the director of CSIS in a memo that source "Winnie the Pooh" had been arrested for drugs and weapons charges. As a very public example, it is widely reported the Americans relied a great deal on an agent they named Curveball for their intelligence on Iraq. Totally understandable that an American agent would have a name from America's sporting pastime. However, I'm not sure if I would have let that one through. It seems like this source didn't exactly "set the record straight," and the name was clearly a little too on the nose. I would love to talk to the American HSP analyst and see if he or she didn't know this one was going to come back to bite them.

You could sometimes tell when people got their code names by what they were named—for example, popular movies might inspire the choices. I assume every pilot call sign in the movie *Top Gun* worked for the Service in 1986. There are probably some Marvel references that have made it in the past few years. It was a great Friday afternoon activity. All the HSP analysts would gather in a bullpen and come up with ridiculous code names, making the rest of the team laugh with the suggestions. Unfortunately, I didn't have the final say. I'd have to submit my list to a team of administrators in the filing office. They were the final authority. I tried to get "Burgundy" and "Anchorman" assigned to human sources with no luck. But I did manage to sneak a couple of fun ones through and got to cheer for them as they advanced in their careers. Any human source who I got to name felt like a child of mine. I wanted them to succeed and do great things. I took great pride when I had to write a memo to the director on one of the human sources I'd named. It may sound sad, but at that point, that was my biggest contribution to the operations.

I'm sure you're wondering, Did I keep up with my French, and did it come in handy? Well, I got lucky that my officemates were Francophones, so they handled all the French memos. Occasionally when they were out and a French message was in our communal email, I would rush into my boss's office and exclaim something along the lines of, "We got a message from Quebec. I can't understand if the bomb went off or is going to go off imminently or is repeatedly going off! Is it the *plus de parfait* or the *passé composé*?"

On one occasion when my co-workers were gone for the day, I got a message that said a subject of investigation had "*défilé de voiture.*" This sounded serious. In my rough translation, someone had defiled a car. My immediate thought was, How does someone even do that? That sounded gross and something I might need to write a memo about. I needed to confirm, so I awkwardly walked into my boss's office for the proper translation. Mercifully she informed me the source had merely participated in a parade. Awesome—memo averted. But she was now herself confused. As I turned to walk out, she asked me, "Andrew, what does 'defiled a car' mean in English?"

"Um, nothing we'd want in a code name," is all I could think to respond.

Don't Believe Everything You Read

It was definitely an interesting experience, being a policy compliance officer for my first post at CSIS. It was extremely rare to have a case where policy was contravened deliberately or flagrantly. I was more of a reviewer and report-quality control. Occasionally I would get into debates about the finer points of the rules with the field investigators, who often didn't appreciate having me nitpick their plans and source reports. I had final authority, but they had all the real-world experience. In their minds they were doing the heavy lifting and I was slowing them down or causing an unnecessary administrative burden. In my mind I was keeping them (or getting them) out of trouble.

On one occasion an infamously high-strung mid-level manager stormed into one of my HSP colleague's offices to berate him for a policy decision he had made. He got right into his face and started yelling, "I don't know who the fuck you think you are, Anthony! I've been doing this job for twenty years and you don't know what the fuck you're talking about! You got that, Anthony?"

He had a valid policy argument, but it was greatly undermined by the fact the guy he was yelling at was named Michael. Needless to say, from that moment on we all called Mike Anthony.

There was a full policy transformation occurring while I was in the policy shop. CSIS was created in 1984 and some of the rules were clearly held over from a previous time. Most were administrative and procedural. Some of the minor policy annoyances we felt ate up a lot of our time unnecessarily were updated to be more operational, and some policies turned into looser guidelines, which added flexibility. There was still oversight and accountability but an acknowledgement that times change.

One example was texting. Is texting an electronic communication like email or a verbal conversation like a phone call? This might seem like a minor difference, but in policy there were rules about how and when someone could communicate with someone "electronically." For a number of reasons, communicating through emails required more authority than picking up the phone and calling someone. Obviously subscribing to a newsletter or engaging with someone online just wasn't a consideration or concern in the late 1980s. That had to be reconciled with how modern intelligence officers were communicating and engaging with their sources.

Another debate we had was over gift cards. Are gift cards cash? Or are they a gift? There were separate approvals required to give someone money in the form of cash than there were to give someone a tangible gift, like a bottle of wine at Christmas. As an investigator you could buy someone a coffee. If you did it with a Tim Hortons gift card and let them keep the card, you may have been in violation of policy.

In January 2011, just as I was wrapping up my time on the human source policy desk, Canadian Press reported on the CSIS inspector general's audit from 2010, covering international activities for the period from April 2008 to October 2009. The *Globe and Mail* stated the review "uncovered policy violations" and was "the latest indication of shortcomings at the branch that oversees growing operations in foreign hotspots." In May 2012, the title of a *National Post* article covering another inspector general's report stated, "CSIS Regularly Violates Policy, Makes Errors That Could Hurt Effectiveness: Watchdog."

I admit I was pretty sensitive to any reporting that suggested CSIS was breaking rules with abandon. When any inspector general's report came out, I thought about writing a letter to the newspaper to give my side of the story. I wanted to explain how when a human source was recruited, there was a policy that stated the investigator must submit an annual report. Occasionally someone in the approval chain was away and the report sat in an inbox. I was constantly chasing managers to make sure these reports were submitted on time. Miss it by one day and that's a policy violation. Obviously my letter-to-the-editor idea didn't make it very far. Even typing this now feels a little ridiculous.

I honestly don't bring this example up to complain but to highlight what it was I did for almost two years as a CSIS HQ analyst, and why. I had dreams of fighting terrorism, while instead I was playing *The Price Is Right* over airport chocolates, trying to guess the cost, and writing memos about whether the source handlers could accept the gift under current policy. It wasn't glamorous or at all what I'd expected I'd be doing, but it was my job and I took it seriously. Did we make mistakes? Absolutely. If we didn't, they wouldn't have needed policy compliance officers. I was doing my small part to help CSIS carry out our mandate and protect Canada. I also felt strongly that I was protecting CSIS's reputation. If a source or source operation went bad, it could seriously hurt our credibility. I was determined not to let that happen, and I didn't like when it was implied in the press that we had.

HSP was a slog at times, but the type of access and insight I got into how CSIS worked was a huge positive. I spent all day reading and reviewing source reports. I had broad exposure to an incredibly wide range of CSIS initiatives. I got to see many of the source operations, how they started and how we managed them. I was tasked with assessing the productivity of sources and attempting to make qualitative and quantitative evaluations of their motivations and trustworthiness. It was invaluable knowledge to have and prepared me well for when I was eventually unleashed into the field.

Online Dating from Off the Grid

While I was doing all this administrative work, I was also settling into Ottawa as a single man. The nice thing about working in a support role at CSIS is that it was mostly an 8:30-to-4:30 job and did leave time on the evenings and weekends for a social life. I tried to make it a point to look outwards for that—CSIS can be a little incestuous. I saw it in training and I only saw more of it as I started on my desk. I can't tell you statistically; it felt like there was slightly more coupling at CSIS than in my previous jobs but slightly less than at summer camp. I stayed away from office romances. I made a point of it. I know many happy couples from CSIS; I just personally liked having some separation in my life. Dating someone at work brought worlds together and I liked keeping them apart.

So, where does a spy find love if it isn't at work? This spy found it on the internet. Now is that the most safe and secure way to meet someone? Absolutely not, but I was a bit of a homebody, I liked online dating and I was pretty good at it. I tried all the sites: Jdate, Plenty of Fish, Eharmony. This predates the current crop of dating apps like Tinder and Bumble.

I had been online dating before I joined CSIS, when I'd moved back to Toronto from London. It was where I met my long-distance girlfriend. And before her I'd gone on a number of pretty good dates that hadn't ended up working out for a variety of reasons. There had been one very attractive Jewish woman from Montreal. She worked in marketing at McDonald's Canada. On our second date, we had a nice time at Carens, a wine bar in Yorkville. She was tough to read, but at the end of the night I pressed my luck and kissed her on the street while she was waiting for her taxi to arrive. It was a Tuesday night and the usually picturesque Yorkville street was lined with piles of garbage bags ready for collection. It was a decent kiss but not in the most romantic of settings. I kicked myself for forcing the moment and ending the date on that awkward note. I liked her. She never called me back.

I liked to think that I had matured quite a bit since then. I was also now gainfully employed, living on my own and literally trained in recruiting people, which I thought would help. Of course, now it was a little different. There was absolutely a conflict between trying to keep a low profile and online dating. It wasn't banned at work, but it was frowned upon. So, I was cautious. I was suspicious of women I didn't know or have friends in common with. Honey traps are real. Online dating is sketchy. I didn't want to become a case study for future training classes.

To make matters worse, in Ottawa you can't just write "government" as an occupation on your profile and expect people to gloss over it. Ottawa is a true government town. The main career diversity would be between the public servants and the political staffers. If I ran into someone who asked me what I was up to, I would generally tell them that I worked for the government writing policy and try to bore them. It worked very, very well in Toronto. In Ottawa, once I acknowledged I was in government, it sparked a lot of questions.

The first giveaway is the Government Electronic Directory Services (GEDS). If I worked for the government, I should be on GEDS. Of course, I wasn't on GEDS, so it struck people as a little unusual. The other giveaway was my position level. If I worked for the government, I should have a unionized, management or executive position level or designation. I did not have any such thing. I learned I needed to make one up pretty quickly as I got asked about it *all the time*. At first I was a little surprised, since asking someone what their level was would pretty quickly give away someone's salary range or seniority. I didn't think that was something people talked about. Turns out in Ottawa, next to the weather and traffic, it's one of the main things people talk about.

It was a fine dance with strangers and one-off acquaintances I met at a party or a friend's gathering. I could make stuff up or be slightly rude to people I was never going to see again. For the purposes of dating, though, I was hoping to see these people again. In some cases, I wouldn't be able to help it. Ottawa is a small town. A lot of people have friends or know someone who works at CSIS.

I could get a sense pretty early on if someone knew and was looking for confirmation. There is a different tone between someone's interest in your job and someone trying to catch you in a lie. If I got asked directly, I would just say, "Obviously if I worked there, I wouldn't be able to talk about it." That worked a lot better than having an extensive back and forth with someone who was accusing me of being a spy and me adamantly proclaiming that I wasn't. Those weren't great first dates and never led to a second.

One of the more conflicted experiences I had online dating in Ottawa was finding out a girl I was going on a date with was an exotic dancer. Her Jdate profile said she was a graduate student, and like me she was struggling to meet nice Jewish singles in a town with a small Jewish community. We were on the phone making a plan to get together one night when she told me she was "about to go on stage." "Are you in the theatre?" I asked. "Not exactly."

She explained that she was paying for her classes by dancing at a gentlemen's club over the border in Gatineau. It was a little surprising and not the image I had from her profile pics or our previous conversations. She was cute and very sweet, so I thought, Why not? We met for a coffee the next morning. She wanted to pay, and she pulled out a huge wad of fives, tens and twenties. I didn't need to be a field agent to piece it together. We had a nice time and went on a second date for dinner a couple days later. She had a good sense of humour and was pretty upfront and honest about things, which is more than I could say. I liked her. It was a small town and a smaller pool of Jewish women, so it was nice to meet someone I hit it off with.

It wasn't until a goodnight kiss at the end of our date that the complications of my career began to weigh on me. I didn't feel comfortable inviting her back to my place. I didn't think she was a honey trap or involved in any criminal activity, but she was at the very least criminal adjacent, due not to her work as a dancer but to the industry she worked in. For those who don't follow Canadian politics closely, this was right around the time foreign affairs minister Maxime Bernier's relationship with Julie Couillard led him to resign his post. His error was leaving classified documents in his ex's apartment. The scandal was in part because of her known past associations. If I were in a different career, I wouldn't have thought twice about it. That just wasn't the case. It's a requirement and at times a sacrifice of the job that we are expected to limit our vulnerability to exploitation or pressure. Online dating was borderline—this would have been irresponsible. It would be hard for me to plead ignorance if anything went sideways. I was a full intelligence officer now. I was past the point of bringing in donuts. We were only on date number two and I felt like that was just as far as it could go. Now it was my turn to not call back.

5

IN THE FIELD

————————

AFTER TWO YEARS behind the desk in headquarters, I received my transfer to the Toronto regional office. I was due to report in February 2011. It was the fastest anyone from my training class who had started their career in Ottawa made it out to a region.

CSIS is divided into six regions: Toronto, Ottawa, Quebec, BC, Prairie and Atlantic. In each region there is a main regional office and some smaller district offices. In Quebec region, for example, Montreal is the main regional office and there's a district office in Quebec City. Some district offices can be pretty small. There's one dude just hanging out by himself in Newfoundland. I had dreams of applying for that role and calling myself the Atlantic District Commander.

People were both happy for me and, I'm sure, a little jealous. I was lucky. It's all about "releasability." Your senior management essentially owned you. It was their decision whether to approve a transfer request or hold out until they were able to secure another individual to take your place. Mobility rules all. Many people on high-tempo desks were not released until their management was forced to relent. There were some people from my class who had to wait four years for their transfer. Their management didn't want to lose their expertise or have an empty spot on their team for fear it wouldn't get filled. I, however, was very releasable from the policy shop.

I once again took full advantage of the government relocation assistance program. I sold my place in Ottawa and bought a small condo in downtown Toronto near the CSIS regional office. Even with a good government job and relocation expenses covered, Toronto was expensive, and my mom had to be a guarantor on my mortgage. At the time CSIS offered a "transition allowance" for IOs moving from Ottawa to more expensive jurisdictions like Vancouver and Toronto. The benefit was designed to be a temporary adjustment. It was clawed back over time, so after an initial bump when I moved, my annual overall salary actually went down each year for the first three years I lived in Toronto. As supposed "assistance," it didn't make a lot of sense—it's not like the cost of living in Toronto also reduced over that time. I didn't care. I was just so happy to be home.

What's in a Name?

My first day, in addition to my access card, I was also carrying my CSIS badge with me through those doors. I'd received it the day of graduation, and it had sat in my office safe ever since. Other desk analysts had meetings with law enforcement or other agencies, foreign and domestic, with whom we cooperated. Not me. I'd worn a suit to work every day except casual Fridays, but I'd never met anyone. Nobody outside the Service had ever seen my ties or my badge. When I got my transfer, I pulled it out and dusted it off. Not only was I going to be carrying my badge around, but I would be showing it to people.

It should surprise nobody (and therefore I should be able to disclose it here) to learn that we did not always work in the field under our given names. Like most intelligence officers I had an alias that I could use when I needed to obscure my true identity. It was a name that I got to choose, so in the middle of training we were asked to submit a few options for review. These names were searched in a variety of databases to make sure there wouldn't be any problems. One name I submitted came back from a criminal record check as a serious child sex offender. We didn't want names with red flags that might cause problems in the field, so that name was vetoed. I also made a mental note, should I come across anyone with that name in my life.

I am fortunate that my first name, Andrew, is generic enough and I didn't need or want to change it. It obviously helps to use your real first name. It made it easy for me to remember, but, more importantly, it helped my colleagues remember it as well. Not everyone at CSIS does use their first name for their alias. If you have a unique first name, you might want to change it. I had a few colleagues I used to do joint interviews with who had different first names and I had to constantly remind myself to use them. I'd go into the interview repeating it to myself, "Don't forget to call them [their alias] ... don't forget to call them [their alias] ..." Inevitably, sometimes I would forget, and I'd refer to my colleague by their real name and get a puzzled look from the person we were interviewing. It happens.

In a bit of an ironic twist, a colleague I worked pretty closely with shared the same real first name as me. We would knock on a door and introduce ourselves as Andrew and Andrew from CSIS. We got more than one dubious look, and one hostile interview subject looked at us and said, "You guys couldn't make up two different names?" As I said, I assume most people thought our names were fake, and this guy also thought my partner and I were particularly lazy.

In picking my last name I also wanted something generic. It was important that I didn't have any ethnic affiliation that I couldn't explain. If I had a very Irish-sounding name like O'Malley and I was speaking to someone who was Irish, they may want to talk about family origins. That wasn't something I wanted to have to talk about. This honestly wasn't a huge challenge for me, though. I am a somewhat bland white guy. But I am Jewish. I used to joke in the office that I wanted the alias Shlomo Horowitz. I would pretend to knock on a door and introduce myself: "Shalom, my name is Shlomo Horowitz and I'd like to talk to you about Islamist extremism ..." Obviously that might have been problematic.

At the end of the rigorous selection process, the name I chose was as vanilla as it comes. Nobody ever asked me the ethnic origins of my name. I don't look particularly Jewish, and the name helped mask any awkwardness or stigma that being Jewish might cause. I know that persons of colour from diverse backgrounds did have to find a way to address their ethnicity with a name and backstory that made sense. There was also often the added concern that in some places where there are strong, sometimes opposed, sub-ethnic groups within a community, they would need to find a name and story that would cut across lines and be inoffensive to both groups. Finally, and not insignificantly, my name started with the same letters as my real last name. In the off chance I was ever asked to sign something, it was important that I had some similar letters so if I made a mistake, I could hopefully catch myself and fix it on the fly with minimal confusion. Once again, it happens.

The alias is an important measure we are able to use to put some distance between our work life and personal life. We are trying to build relationships of trust, but there are security considerations for both parties. The idea is that we keep our work relationships confidential for the people we meet as well as for ourselves. We are asked to meet so many people, and we don't want them all trying to google us or add us on LinkedIn. This is for our own personal security, and also because we owe them our discretion and protection from being associated with us. That said, I did work closely with a number of human sources and contacts who I would consider friends, and I would have been comfortable with them knowing my real name. For their own safety, though, we still shouldn't have been Facebook friends.

A Captive Audience

My first stop in the Toronto office was in the security screening branch. Screening is a big part of CSIS's operations and mandate. The Service is tasked with providing background checks on almost everyone who requires security clearance to access classified information or restricted sites such as airports or nuclear facilities, as well as immigration screening for individuals applying for Canadian citizenship. There is an exception for the RCMP, who do their own screening.

The aim of the screening is to determine the loyalty of the subject as well as reliability as it relates to loyalty. Does the individual have any pressures that would make them unreliable and therefore cause them to not be loyal to Canada? Could they be blackmailed because of something they've done? For example, do they have significant debts that would put financial pressure on them and make them susceptible to compromise? In earlier times there was a sensitivity about homosexuality. Now the concern was not lifestyle but the individual's openness about it. Being gay was not an issue. However, if someone was hiding that fact and could be blackmailed to keep it a secret, that could be a problem.

The initial screening involving a file review and database checks is done at headquarters by a large, dedicated team of screening analysts. This includes intelligence officers. The screening branch recruits heavily out of training classes. It's not a particularly desirable or popular spot. It didn't make my top six list of options, and knowing what I do now, I still would have taken my spot in HSP over security screening. They're always busy and the work can get monotonous.

These screeners are identifying potential issues. Let's say we find out the person in question was believed to be in touch with a subject of one of our investigations. Is that because they are friends, or because this person works at a pizza shop the subject of investigation regularly order pies from? These are the kinds of incidental contacts and connections I was consciously trying to avoid by not pursing a relationship with the exotic dancer. There is nothing wrong with visiting a gentleman's club. However, if a subject of investigation for us or the police was a co-worker or regular patron (which could be a distinct possibility), I didn't want to show up in a report every time I picked her up from work.

The initial database checks are done at headquarters. If a follow-up interview is required, that is done by regional investigators. Each regional office has a pool of specialized security screening investigators who do screening interviews as their full-time job. It is helpful to have dedicated investigators because they also do the background checks for CSIS employees, and it would be awkward to work with the person who also did your background check. To supplement this pool of investigators, new intelligence officers were often placed on the screening team, when there was a surge of non-CSIS screening applications and as a way to give the new IOs an opportunity to conduct interviews in a controlled setting. This is what they did with me when I first showed up in Toronto.

It was a great way to start out. The interview subjects were what we would call captive audiences. I would eventually spend a lot of time as an investigator trying to track people down, but screening interviewees were pretty much guaranteed to show up. They also had to talk to you if they wanted their status or security clearance.

I would arrange the interview with the individual and show up with my badge and security booklet. In the case of government screening the questions were set out in advance. Since I already had the script, I could practice my delivery and work on reading visual cues while evaluating the subject's response. I obviously knew the line of questioning and got pretty good at picking my spots for emphasis or a pause for dramatic effect. Most of the questions were innocuous, but some were guaranteed to elicit a reaction. I would go through them routinely... "Do you maintain close associates abroad?" "Do you have any undeclared debts?" "Have you ever been fired from a job?" I'd take my notes, engage in some light banter, get them relaxed and then hit them with what I knew was a whopper... "And what do you look at online?"

Now think for a second about what you look at online. It's a tough question. How does that make you feel? Would you be honest if a stranger asked you that question? And before you think that question is unfair, just know that I got asked some pretty personal questions too when I was hooked up to the polygraph.

Depending on the subject and how the interview was going, this is where I might take a dramatic pause. Maybe put down my pencil or something. The typical answer I got was, "I read the news." Most people would admit to being on social media like Facebook and Twitter, or they would say they play video games. Anything missing? Well, very few people admit to watching pornography online. Yet Pornhub.com is in the top ten websites visited in all the world. It's also Canadian, and the only Canadian site in the top ten. Yay Canada.

The aim wasn't to embarrass someone but to determine reliability. It's quite conceivable that someone's online viewing habits could make them vulnerable to blackmail. But how far do you want to go with that? I certainly didn't go too far. Honestly, I was just as uncomfortable asking the question as the person receiving it was. Well, maybe not quite as uncomfortable.

I used it as an opportunity for what I thought was fair warning. To paraphrase, I'd ask, "Do you watch anything that you would be uncomfortable with other people knowing about?" or, "If you were confronted with someone threatening to release your online viewing habits to someone close to you, would you betray your country?" I didn't need to know the ins and outs of what that was. I just wanted to drive that point home.

The second question that usually aroused some hesitant responses was about drug use. Marijuana is legal now, but it wasn't at the time. It was generally assumed that people did drugs. I asked that question once and someone looked at me and sheepishly said, "I'm from British Columbia!" As if drug use was implied. I turned to that person and deadpanned, "Please just answer the question."

Once again, the issue is reliability. Is the person honest? I wasn't there to bust anyone for pot but to know if frequent drug use could put the person in a compromising position. Do you get blackout drunk and wake up in strange places? Are you open about it? If you remember the training exercise where I had to chat up a stranger, my new friend in the Irish pub wasn't drinking. A few of my classmates found some liquored up chatty Cathys who were very happy to share sensitive details about their work. If they had access to classified information, that could be a problem.

Immigration screening was a little different. CSIS works with Immigration, Refugees and Citizenship Canada (IRCC) and the Canada Border Services Agency (CBSA) to do immigration and citizenship screening. CSIS and CBSA provide security advice to IRCC to make sure applicants are not a threat to national security. CSIS would be looking for issues that would lead to inadmissibility to the country, such as ties to banned organizations. In some cases, information would come up in a background check that would need to be addressed, and the threat would have to be evaluated with an interview. (It's important to note that CSIS does not make decisions on applications. The IRCC makes the final decisions.)

Working in security screening was a good way to practise asking questions, listening for the answers and then following up. It was indeed a captive audience, but it was artificial and not very indicative of how future interviews would go out in the field. I appreciated the fact that these people wanted something from me rather than vice versa. It was in their interest to be nice, to talk, to appear to answer questions even if they didn't want to or didn't have good answers. I had leverage. In future conversations, I would have much less.

It was also my first introduction to how nervous I, or we at CSIS, could make people just by our position and the context of the conversation. I could have a very nice interview with someone: I would go through my checklist, not have too much controversial material to cover and have what I thought was a pleasant and non-confrontational conversation. But at the end I would shake the person's hand and they'd be incredibly sweaty and clammy. It was like they'd just washed their hands and hadn't dried them.

It was something I had to constantly remind myself of throughout my career. I may be a very nice person and our chat may be collegial, but there would always be a power imbalance and that person could be very tense or even afraid just being in my presence. I assume police officers have to keep this in mind all the time, but the fact they are wearing a uniform and possibly carrying a gun makes that power imbalance quite clear. In my case, I was unarmed and often dressed the exact same as the person I was talking to.

After a couple of months, I got the call. The volume in screening was low and a spot had opened up on a regional desk carrying out operational investigations.

My First Cold Call

For those still reading, I know what you may be thinking. You're well into this book about my life as a spy and I haven't actually done anything you might consider "spying" yet. What you're feeling now,

I felt it too. I'd applied online to CSIS in March 2006 in a haze of patriotism and a call to service. In my first recruitment interview I was quizzed on the CSIS Act and mandate. Finally, I would be carrying out its core function and collecting information on threats to the security of Canada. I had worked my way out of headquarters, through screening and finally onto an operational field desk. I felt it was like being called up to the major leagues. I was nervous and incredibly excited. It was now March 2011, and I was about to knock on my first door as Andrew [REDACTED], regional investigator for the Canadian Security Intelligence Service.

I was placed with an operational team that was responsible for investigating threats related to a geographic area including parts of the Middle East and North Africa. Remember, we don't have a foreign intelligence service, so we weren't investigating countries themselves. Rather, our desk was simply responsible for any threats that were related or in some way connected to the area geographically, whether due to a domestic target's nationality or a terrorist entity base of operation in that region. Desk organization and reorganization was a constant at CSIS. It would flip back and forth between geographic areas and then threat-specific investigations. Sometimes they would merge, then split out again.

My first tasking on the desk was pretty straightforward. There was an individual from Turkey who was believed to be associated with the Kurdistan Workers' Party (PKK). The PKK has been listed by Public Safety Canada as a terrorist organization. This person was known to CSIS. We believed that he had returned to Turkey months earlier and was no longer in Toronto. However, someone in the community had reported seeing him recently, and it was my job to check if he was still out of town.

I was handed this tasking by my supervisor without any further discussion or explanation. I have to admit I was a little nervous. Some IO-training graduates go straight on to being regional investigators. This group of IOs is called "direct to regions." It's not a creative name but it does signify that they haven't had experience at headquarters. My HQ experience was valuable in understanding how CSIS worked, but I had never knocked on a door before. The direct-to-regions IOs are provided with a little more hand holding when they get to the field. I, however, was expected to be a fully functional investigator since I was already more than two years into my career. I was on my own.

I knew from a brief review of the file that the guy I was interested in lived in the basement apartment of a family home. I got to the house and knocked on the door to his apartment. I remember being very uncomfortable. I had no idea how this was going to go. In training, when I'd read the scenarios and prepped for role playing, I'd had a general idea of what information I was interested in and loose goals for the conversation. Build rapport, ask questions, et cetera. Now I didn't feel like I had any sort of objective, or anything to ask about. I was literally just going to check if he was home. I didn't really know what I was going to do if he was.

Mercifully, there was no answer at his door. I looked around for a mailbox to see if there was any mail in his name to that address. Nothing. I went to the main door of the house. I assumed the people who lived there knew him. He was their tenant, after all. I didn't know if they were close friends or relatives. From the names it seemed as though they were from the same ethnic background. That happens a lot: people move to Canada and find accommodations with a family friend or someone in the community they know and trust.

I knocked on the front door and a young woman answered. She looked about the age of a university student. I didn't introduce myself or show any identification. I said I was sorry to bother her, but I was looking for the person downstairs. She said he'd moved out months ago to go home, and she didn't think he was coming back anytime soon. I thanked her and apologized again for bothering her. I turned and started walking away. She called out to me, "Excuse me, what is this about?"

I thought about just ignoring her and continuing on, but I was still so close it would have seemed impossible not to hear her calling out to me. I knew the individual was in the process of applying or had applied for some sort of immigration status. I am not sure if it was refugee, permanent residence or citizenship. I turned and said, "I'm from the government, checking to confirm an address from an immigration application." I turned back around and quickened my pace. I didn't say what department I was from, but I certainly implied it was an immigration matter and that's who I was representing. She accepted my excuse, and I hurried back into my car before she could press me further.

I beat myself up a bit on the ride back to the office. Why did I even need to invoke another Canadian department? Why hadn't I brought a package with me? I could have said I was a courier and looking for the individual for a delivery. No, that wouldn't have worked—what if he had been home? Was it wrong to imply I was from immigration? I hadn't lied. I mean, I was CSIS... I could be covert or clandestine, right? Isn't that how it's supposed to work? Oh shoot, I thought next, I didn't get the person's name. Should I have asked for the young woman's name? Would she have given it to me? She'd given me the information about the guy I was looking for; did I need to know who *she* was?

The address check went about as well as one could go, and yet I was relentlessly second-guessing myself. And when I say it went as well as it could go: I was able to corroborate our previous reporting that the person had left months ago from someone who was believed to have direct knowledge of the individual's plans. I made some notes in the car and returned to the office to write up my first regional report. I now had a door knock under my belt. It was a baptism for any new CSIS regional investigator. I definitely had things I wanted to work on in my approach and pretexts. I would have a lot of opportunities to practice.

6

NEW TO
THE COMMUNITY

I N THOSE early days I was mostly doing address checks and some
random one-off information-gathering assignments where I got to
practise introducing myself as Andrew from CSIS. It was definitely
a little strange at first, especially since I was now back in Toronto trying to work discreetly in the city where I'd grown up and most of my
family still lived. The odds of running into people I knew in Ottawa
were small. Toronto was a much larger city but there were many more
people who knew me there. They were like hidden landmines, and
avoiding them added a little more stress to my new undercover life.

I am very close with my family and would see them every weekend. I wasn't able to tell them much about what I was doing beyond
the fact that I knocked on doors and talked to people. They didn't
know my alias, my geographic area of focus or anyone I worked with.
They knew where I worked, and that was enough—they didn't press
me for details I wasn't able to share.

I had gone away to university, lived abroad in London and then
moved to Ottawa. Most of my Toronto friends weren't necessarily
used to having me around. A few knew where I worked. Most didn't.

I found myself gravitating to work colleagues in Toronto more than I had in Ottawa. I typically liked to separate my work and personal life, but I found a lot of comfort being surrounded socially by people I could speak to openly about the unique stresses and challenges of the job. It was awkward to run into old friends and have to fumble through an answer about where I had been and what I was doing now.

The distinction of my two lives was brought much more into focus being back home. All day long I would be running around the city introducing myself as an investigator from CSIS, and at night and on weekends, to people from my real life, I was a make-believe government bureaucrat. With the exception of my name, I was doing far more lying in my real life, which was definitely one reason I gravitated more to the people who knew me by my fake one.

After about a month on my regional desk I got my first formal project: investigating the threat of terrorism in Canada by members or associates of Al Qaeda (AQ) in Iraq. To put this in perspective and proper context, in 2007 the United States escalated its presence in Iraq by deploying additional troops in an effort to enhance security. This surge and the subsequent years did have a positive effect, and by 2011 a lot of information that had been gathered from military operations in the country was starting to come out. Our desk was receiving a steady stream of intel from our American friends on Canadians and people with ties to Canada who might also have connections to Al Qaeda and those involved in the conflict in Iraq.

Our concerns were that Al Qaeda could use supporters in Canada to fundraise or provide material assistance to the war in Iraq. Or worse, members of the terrorist organization could conduct attacks in Canada or use Canada as a base of operations for attacks in the United States. These leads and these threats were now my responsibility.

The challenge I faced with this assignment was that the majority of the potentially threat-related information was completely impossible to track down in its current form. It could be as obscure as "Ali (LNU) from Toronto is believed to be in touch with members of AQ in Iraq." In some cases, the information was about people who had possible ties to AQ wanting to come to Canada. They weren't even here yet.

Quick clarification: "LNU" means "last name unknown." If we knew a first name but not a last name, we would say "Andrew (LNU)." It is pronounced "lenu" or "linu." Similarly, for first names, "FNU" stands for "first name unknown." The woman who had told me that the tenant wasn't home was a "Finu Linu."

Another issue was that when there was concrete information, there often wasn't any context provided on the nature or severity of the threat. "Phone number (416) 555-XXXX was believed to be in contact with persons associated with AQ in Iraq." What does "persons associated" mean? Were the people here a threat? Were the people they were in touch with a threat?

Basically, I was handed a list of broken leads and people who may or not be identifiable. And even if they were, I didn't have any concrete information that would specifically tie them to threat-related activities as defined by the CSIS Act.

My supervisor had been in CSIS for a while. We sat down and assessed the challenge of tracking down these leads. We couldn't ignore the information we had already received and the likelihood we would get more. A trusted contact or human source would likely be the first person we would bring this list to, to ask them for input. They might say, "Oh, I know so-and-so, don't worry about them," or that it looked like an individual who had recently moved here, and they would then go find out more. At that time, we did not have a suitably strong network in the Iraqi community we could consult with for support and assistance. I was tasked with developing one.

There is a misconception that CSIS only talks to people who are in trouble or close to people of concern. That is very far from the truth. We rely on sentinel contacts who are leaders in their community. We are constantly looking for those who have wide networks and associations. We want to know the people who know who's who and what's going on.

These community contacts aren't in trouble and generally appreciate CSIS talking to them and looking to them for advice and guidance on what is happening. Many communities are extremely close-knit, and if individuals come into the community who are not who they appear to be, or someone acts out and may be of concern, these leaders will be the first to know about it. They are invaluable in helping understand the community, for raising concerns to CSIS, and they can advise on any issues that we bring to them.

Over the next year I spent most of my time as a regional investigator trying to solicit assistance from the ninety-nine percent who were honest and good people while I tried to track down the one percent who were up to no good. I got much more comfortable in my investigator role, talking to people and collecting information. These aren't high-stakes negotiations over baccarat and cocktails at a casino. It's much less glamorous. I was in the coffee-and-conversations business.

One thing some people may not consider, but is actually key, is *how* to approach someone. There aren't hard and fast rules; every person and situation is different. The two general approaches are a cold call—knocking on someone's door at home, work or somewhere else you know they will be, but they don't know you're coming—or, alternatively, phoning them in advance and arranging a time and place to meet. There is no way to know how someone will react to a request to meet from CSIS. For most Canadians it's not every day their domestic intelligence service wants to talk to them. I've seen some people panic and others so calm that it was a little unnerving.

I started out with a cold call approach. The benefit of a cold call is that I could manage the interview subject's reaction in person. I would knock on their door and, if they were home, show them my badge, put a non-threatening face to the name of the organization and be there to reassure them that everything was all right and they weren't in trouble. Most importantly I could speak to them about what I needed to talk to them about before they had a chance to talk to other people. I always wanted to keep these conversations confidential, and when I met them for the first time in person, I could stress that on the spot and read the person to get a sense of whether they understood what I was asking for.

Of course, I ended up knocking on a lot of doors when people weren't home. I might try that one or two times before I gave up the element of surprise and tried calling in advance to set up the meeting. I also felt scheduling a meeting was a more respectful and less confrontational approach. I always had in the back of my mind the sweaty palms of my security screening interviewees, as well the experience my friend had when CSIS arrived at his new job for my reference check. Most people don't like to be surprised at home or at work by a visit from the government. I appreciated that it could be stressful to have someone from CSIS show up at your door and ask to talk. They may understand the situation, but it can cause some grief. Building rapport and trust, and establishing confidentiality, were the key goals of the first meeting. This would be harder if a first impression involved embarrassing them or making them feel uncomfortable in front of family or colleagues.

Calling someone up and asking to meet with them somewhere discreet wasn't without its own challenges. In the age of CRA scams, you can imagine that telling someone over the phone that you're from CSIS and asking to go for coffee doesn't always go over smoothly. A lot of the time they just don't believe you at first. If they do believe you, the person will want to know, "Who is this *really*?" "*What* do you want to talk about?" and "Why do you want to talk to *me*?" Typically, we can't get into all of that on the phone. The aim of the call is to get the meeting. It's hard to assuage concerns, prove legitimacy and explain what you want on the phone. There's an expression in politics, "If you're explaining, you're losing." At CSIS, if you're explaining and negotiating over the phone, you're in trouble.

When I'd call someone, I'd stress that I thought they could be of assistance to a national security investigation. I would always try to be accommodating and respectful and stress the need for confidentiality. It still didn't always go smoothly. Sometimes I'd hang up the phone and find out later the person's next call would be to a lawyer, a friend, the police or even the person I wanted to talk to them about. I might get a phone call back from a lawyer trying to get answers, or worse, have company show up at the meeting I wasn't expecting. Unless it was urgent, I also never called someone on a Friday. If they couldn't meet that day they'd stress about it all weekend long. Guaranteed they would confide in someone over the weekend and confidentiality was gone.

Every phone call or cold call could be its own adventure. One time I stopped in on someone at work. He seemed happy to chat but asked if I wouldn't mind meeting him at the Tim Hortons just down the street. He didn't want to have a conversation at his office where other people could overhear. I agreed and drove down the street. As I was waiting at the Tim Hortons, I saw his car speed right by me like he was in a car chase. He was not coming to meet me but basically fleeing. I gave him a call and asked him what he was doing. He said he was sorry, but he didn't want to speak to me after all. He clearly had just sent me to Tim Hortons to get me out of his office. That was a little annoying. I told him as calmly and firmly as I could that I had to speak to him. I had a quick question. He wasn't in trouble, but I needed to ask him something. I said we could either meet at the Tim Hortons that night or I'd come back to his office tomorrow. He pulled a U-turn and made his way back over for a nice chat.

Another time I called up someone who had met with a colleague of mine about a year prior. The notes on the last report suggested he was amenable to speaking further. There hadn't been any activity on the file, so nobody had contacted him in a while. Given his history with the Service and the fact there was no urgency, I thought I would be respectful and call to see when he might be available to chat. On the phone I introduced myself as Andrew from CSIS. I mentioned that I believed he had spoken to my colleague about a year ago and asked if he would meet me for a coffee. He said he was happy to meet with me, but he had never met with anyone from CSIS before. I was confused. I looked quickly at the file. Is this so-and-so? "Yes." Did you meet with so-and-so? "No." He was polite but firm.

I wasn't sure what was happening but thought we could figure it all out when we met. I assume it isn't every day people meet with CSIS, and when we do meet with someone, we generally leave an impression. Anyway, we had a coffee later that week. I showed him my badge and introduced myself. Before I could say anything, he said immediately, "Yes, of course I met with your colleague, but I'm not going to admit that on the phone to someone I've never met!" He was right. I told him it was great operational security. He'd assumed it was a test. It wasn't, but he certainly was proud of himself for passing.

Not everyone was so discreet. In every conversation I would stress confidentiality. I would promise the person that whatever they told me would not be shared, and I asked that anything that we spoke about, and even the fact that we were meeting, be kept quiet. I was giving my standard confidentiality pitch when an interview subject started shaking his head at me. He seemed annoyed. I tried to continue because it was important, and he slammed his hand down on the table.

"Do you know where I am from?" he started. I nodded my head. "You do not need to tell me this! Where I am from, we do not talk about anything. You have no problems with me. Of course, I know this! I would never say anything!" He made such a big show of it. There was a certain irony to him yelling and banging the table at me telling me how discreet he was. The neighbours could probably hear us in the apartment next door, but whatever. He wasn't angry, he was trying to be emphatic. "Of course," I told him. "I don't mean to insult you, but I have to say this. Thank you so much."

The very next day I got a phone call from another investigator in the region. Apparently, my interview subject had been down at the cultural centre for an event that night. He had told everyone and their children that he had met with CSIS. He even showed my business card around. By coincidence, there was another community contact at the event, and he let the person he spoke to at CSIS know, who then gave me a call. I said thanks for the heads-up. It was just a community interview, so I wasn't worried about what he said. In fact, it would have been great if some of his friends had given me a call and asked to talk. I should have given him more cards. Unfortunately, I could never see the guy again. Or rather, I couldn't discuss anything of importance with him. Not everyone should be a human source, or even a community contact.

Once I got a hold of them, most people were happy to speak with me and the Service. There was only one occasion when a casual community contact flatly denied a coffee request. In fact, he got quite angry at even being asked. It was so unexpected and unusual it actually caught me off guard. I kind of blurted out, "You know, everyone I call agrees to meet with me and I didn't think you'd be any different. I just wanted to have a casual conversation. If I'm honest, the fact that you're so against meeting with me is kind of making me a little concerned. Is there anything I need to know about? Is everything okay?" His demeanour changed almost instantly, and he became much more receptive to an interview. We ended up having a nice chat, even meeting a few more times. It turned out he did have something I needed to know about and after the initial shock of getting my call was open to informing us about it.

For these coffee meetings, I'd typically arrive at least twenty minutes early at the pre-determined coffee shop. I wanted to make sure I got a table, preferably one that didn't have too many people nearby. This was ideal but tough to predict twenty minutes before a meeting. Inevitably someone would sit right beside me two minutes before the scheduled time. At the very least, I'd try to keep my back to a wall and have the door in my front view so I could see the person as they entered and see if there were exits that I could get to should I need a quick getaway. Back corner booths were perfect. Being near the bathroom was not—the less traffic the better. This honestly wasn't any kind of super-secret tradecraft; it was just a way to try to ensure some privacy and limit distractions.

I'd get my coffee and sit down at the table. I had a notebook, so I'd take some time to go back over my interview prep notes and think about what information I was looking for and questions I was hoping to get answered. I got in the habit of arriving so early that sometimes I'd panic that I was sitting in the wrong coffee shop or being stood up if the person wasn't right on time. It always felt like I had been there forever when really the person was just running a not-atypical few minutes late.

I didn't always know what the person looked like, nor did they know me. I think all of my experience online dating prepared me well to spot someone entering a coffee shop looking for someone they hadn't met before. It probably helped that I looked exactly as you might expect a man named Andrew (with a super generic white alias) from CSIS to look. I'd lock eyes with my coffee date, and they'd make their way over to my table.

Sometimes they would line up to get their own coffee before joining me and other times they'd sit right down. How quickly they wanted to start our conversation was probably a good indication of how nervous they were to meet. Sitting right down meant they wanted to get on with it; grabbing a coffee indicated a little more comfort with the situation. I'd put my notebook away at that point. I didn't like to have it open or even on the table. I wanted to make them as comfortable as possible and I felt like note-taking made it seem like a formal interview and got in the way of building rapport.

I started every conversation the same way: I introduced myself, showed my badge and explained the CSIS mandate. I got pretty good at flashing my badge discreetly in coffee shops. I had a few different moves, but usually I'd go low beside the table to keep it out of view of other patrons. It was important to identify myself and explain what CSIS was. I'd try to get to the heart of the conversation as soon as possible. While it is a Canadian tradition to talk at length about the weather, every first conversation had a pretty big elephant in the room and I assumed the other person was anxious to know exactly what had brought us together that day.

I explained to them my general concerns in an open and transparent way. CSIS investigates terrorism and we want to make sure that Canadians are not participating in the activities of or aiding terrorist groups in any way. At the time, we were seeing many people leave Iraq and attempt to emigrate to Canada. This was not a secret. Many of the people I met had friends or family members in the immigration process. I explained that we want to make sure that people who come to Canada are not coming to cause trouble or bring any religious or sectarian violence here. I'd get a very strong nod of the head. At that point, we were a team.

Meeting with a community leader was pretty straightforward. I would tell them that they were considered such and I hoped if they saw or heard anything of concern they would let me know. I asked them to be eyes and ears in the community. I tried my best to explain what I was looking for so they could tell me if they saw it.

I struggled the first few times I met with someone on my "Finu Linu" list. I gave them the same overview of my investigation and concerns, but I didn't know how much I should tell them or ask them about the information I had on them personally.

I was largely on my own at this point, knocking on doors and meeting in coffee shops, but there were other investigators on the desk and we had a supervisor we reported to. As I got more comfortable doing my job, I also got better at asking for help and advice from everyone. When I didn't know what I was doing I was embarrassed to admit it. As my confidence grew, so did my willingness to admit when I needed help.

I went to the new supervisor who had taken over the desk to game out some scenarios and help me with my interview approach. We thought I needed to be a little more direct—which was difficult because of how little information I usually had and my discomfort with confrontation. He then gave me a phrase that he used and found worked well to prompt a conversation. I would say to the person very soberly, "Look, I can't tell you why I'm here or what specific information I have, but your name came across my desk, suggesting you might be involved or know people involved in threat-related activities as defined by the CSIS Act. I don't know if these claims are true, but it's my job to follow them up." Then I hit them with, "*Help me close this file.*"

"Help me close this file" really resonated with people. For the pleasers it was like a siren song. They wanted so badly to be helpful and not disappoint. They would tell me whatever they could think I wanted to hear. For those who were a little reluctant or nervous, it was a non-threatening and bureaucratic way to tell someone that they were on the radar of a domestic intelligence service. I thought it was a fair thing to say. And it had the benefit of being true.

The reality was, we *were* together in that moment because I needed information I believed the person across from me had. Even if neither one of us knew what that information was, I wanted to make it clear it was in both our interests to figure it out. It was a great line and I used it liberally.

Learning as I Go

CSIS expects their intelligence officers to be generalists. Just because you may be from a particular background or have language or education experience in an area does not mean that you will necessarily work on that particular subject. The frequent movement between desks and investigations also means investigators are constantly getting up to speed on the threats they cover and the affected communities.

I don't think the people I met expected me to be an expert. After all, that's why I was talking to them. I was in the community openly asking for information and advice. I'd take everything, and community, cultural and societal background information could be incredibly valuable. There were a few moments when I did have to fake it. On more than one occasion someone would be talking about their community or country of origin and look at me and say, "You probably know this." The last thing I wanted to say is yes. For starters, I often didn't. My common refrain would be, "I know some, but I want to know what *you* know about it . . ."

The mystique of CSIS did help me to overcome my lack of advanced knowledge of my geographic area. It's certainly an advantage that everyone thinks we know everything, or that I could at least credibly pretend to. It's a great catch-all when someone says, "How did you get my name and phone number?" I wouldn't have to tell them their neighbour gave it to me. I'd just give them a knowing smile and say, "We're CSIS." But more often than not I didn't pretend to be omniscient.

You might be wondering, well, if I didn't have existing ties in the community, where did all these contact opportunities come from? I'm sure if you've been visited by CSIS you'd like to know. Some are names from partners or other sources. I'd ask every contact I met if there was anyone else they could think of who I should reach out to, promising not to disclose where the lead came from. I found a few names through old-fashioned analysis of information we already had. CSIS has a robust database that you can go into and search. Aside from the many spellings of Saskatchewan, in my time it was reasonably organized and certainly if you knew what you were looking for you would be able to find it. The only challenge back then was that it wasn't particularly good at synthesizing information for you. It was more of a repository rather than a platform that could support complex queries and generate multifaceted reporting. I believe this has since changed. At the time it was a bit of a slog.

It became clear in my research that there had been a previous push on community interviews. The United States had invaded Iraq back in 2003. By around 2005, Iraq was getting ready for parliamentary elections, and as it turned out we had a lot of Iraqi Canadians in Canada with close ties to the burgeoning new government and reconstruction effort. There were also Iraqi Canadians in Iraq who were taking positions of power and influence in the new government. And a lot of them also happened to have close family and friends in Toronto.

This is not unique. People from all over the world have come to Canada when their countries were suffering through conflict or strife. Some return home, many stay, but almost all keep in close contact with people who remain. It just so happened that a very enterprising and diligent CSIS IO in the Toronto region, years before I arrived, had figured out who all those people were. He had interviewed almost all of them. He had informed his management and written reports about it. Then he went on paternity leave for a year. Nobody else cared enough to follow up.

He came back to work and was promptly moved to another desk. His role wasn't replaced. This was the time of domestic extremism and resources were needed to investigate other priorities. The file lay essentially dormant—until we did care again, years later, because the Americans told us "Finu Linu" might be coming to Canada and may know someone connected to Al Qaeda.

I picked up this baton and started to run with it. I was a white, Jewish, private school guy from downtown Toronto running around asking Sunni and Shia Muslim and Assyrian members of the Iraqi diaspora, many of whom were recent immigrants and refugees, to help me find potential supporters of Al Qaeda. I could not have found a more supportive and welcoming community.

The people I met talked about Iraq with affection and regret. I learned from them about the country's political dynamic and the diasporic community here. Many were frustrated that Canada did not have a more active role to play in the Middle East. They kept asking me if I would tell Canada—like it was a person—to do more and care more. Frustrations aside, they had a love for both their home country and their adopted one. They were happy to help any way they could. It wasn't until later I realized that my experience was unique.

I was out one morning with a new person to our desk. She was actually more senior than I was, so it wasn't any sort of mentoring, but just a good opportunity to start knocking on doors and get familiar with the community and one of our files. In this case we were doing a cold call on a woman where there had been some derogatory information about her ex-husband. We did have a name but we didn't really know what the threat was. We assumed the individual's ex-wife would be a good place to start. It was also helpful going to this interview with a female investigator. I thought it would make the interview subject feel more comfortable with us. We didn't have any negative information about her, and even that about her ex wasn't confirmed or corroborated. Nevertheless, we had enough info that we needed to track it down.

I knocked on the door and a very polite woman in maybe her late thirties or early forties let us into her apartment. We explained who we were, and we were welcomed in with the warmth and hospitality I was used to. The woman had been in the country a while. She had recently separated from her husband and was living with their adolescent daughter in the basement of a large, rundown rental building. We were offered drinks and treats and told to make ourselves comfortable on a small couch in the living room.

I took a glass of water and she started boiling some water for tea. After some initial pleasantries our host got up from her chair across from us to go back to the kitchen and bring out the tea. This was not an unusual experience for me, so I didn't think twice. My partner turned to me and said in a low and concerned tone, "What the fuck is happening right now?"

I couldn't help but laugh. My partner had just joined our team from what was a bit of a multi-issue extremism catch-all desk that included left-wing and right-wing militants. I can't remember if her particular area was the anarchists, what today we might call Antifa, or right-wing terrorism. Regardless, to say that this was not the greeting she was used to would be an understatement. Her interview subjects were often rude, aggressive and potentially violent people.

She was never invited in. She was usually berated on the front door-step by someone ranting about how the government is evil, she was a tool of the state and they felt violated by her very presence. That was not my experience at all. While she was getting called every name in the book and worried about getting covertly filmed and having her interview and CSIS identity posted online, I was having pleasant chats and nice cups of tea.

It should be said that female IOs have their own unique challenges that I got to witness first-hand on a couple of occasions on my regional desk. I had been meeting with one community leader for a few months. We had built up a good rapport. He was a professional businessman with a wife and family. We used to grab coffee and talk about the stock market. I was getting transferred to another team and I needed to introduce him to someone to take over.

I brought along a female IO to meet him and his whole demeanour changed. He was suddenly flirty and a little more self-important. I had described him to my colleague as a family man and the guy she met was a leering cad. I introduced them and the first thing out of his mouth was something to the effect of, "Andrew, you didn't say she would be so beautiful." It made me uncomfortable, but she took it in stride. I apologized afterwards. She said she was fine. Nothing she wasn't used to.

On another occasion, I was planning to go out to meet a gentleman I didn't think had a strong grasp of English, so I asked a female colleague who spoke that language to come along. It was my file so we briefed in the car on the way there on what I was looking for so she could conduct the interview and I would be there if anything came up of note. We knocked on the door and the man's wife answered. She also did not speak English, so my colleague took the lead. She showed her badge and told me to show mine. She introduced us and explained what CSIS was. The lady invited us into the house, and we all sat down in the living room.

My colleague and this woman carried on what seemed like a very pleasant conversation. I sat on the couch and tried my best to nod along. They were in a groove, building rapport. It didn't make sense for my colleague to turn to me and do literal translation of everything

thing they were saying. She was an intelligence officer and she was conducting an interview. I just sat there. I looked around the apartment, stared at my bag and smiled occasionally to try to look friendly.

After a pleasant chat the woman got up from the couch and walked into the kitchen. I asked my colleague how things were going. She said great. She'd got a lot of info. The woman was going to call her husband at work and see if he could come home to meet with us. Awesome, I thought. Then I heard the woman in the kitchen say something, and my colleague got a little flustered. She bowed her head and shook it. She was composed but annoyed.

"What's wrong?" I asked.

"It's nothing," she said.

"What did she say?" I pressed on.

Through gritted teeth my colleague looked at me and said, "She told her husband, 'The man from the government is here. And he brought his interpreter with him.'"

It was pretty insulting and a small glimpse into a disrespect that I never had to experience. I'm sure she wished she hadn't told me and had just buried it, like she probably had many times before.

If it was any consolation for my colleague, the joke was on me a few weeks later when it was my turn to experience a case of mistaken identity.

Calling Your Lawyer, or Worse . . . the Cops

With all the cold calls and community interviews we conduct, it's inevitable that every field investigator has the police called on them at least once in their careers. The general public is not familiar with CSIS, so if someone calls you up and tells you they are from the government and they want to meet in a coffee shop, it's understandable if they assume the worst. The police aren't usually the first call. It typically has to do with the background of the person you're speaking with. For example, anyone who is at any stage of the immigration process, upon hearing CSIS wants to meet, will call their immigration lawyer. In fact, if I knew that was the case, I took great pains to explain over the phone that this had nothing to do with their immigration status. It didn't matter. They always called their lawyer.

I've had many friends and neighbours of the interview subject sit in on what were supposed to be private interviews. Sometimes that was just for translating purposes. It's always a little disconcerting when someone you aren't expecting shows up. By that point, I'd typically done a fair amount of background research on the individual in question and any known associates. I'd also spent time prepping for what I wanted to ask the person and who I wanted to talk about. If I didn't know the new meeting participant, I had to reconsider on the fly if the line and subject of questioning was appropriate.

It also is much more difficult to build rapport and trust in a group setting than one on one. Even bringing an interpreter or second CSIS interviewer to a meeting changes the dynamic. Two interviewing one can be more intimidating. We tried to avoid that when we could and limit the chance that anyone we weren't expecting would show up to the meeting. It's the most awkward when that extra person is the police.

One evening I was sent out to get some information that we believed was relevant to an immediate threat to life. This does not happen often. Most of the time investigations can move at their own pace and we are able to be flexible with the people we want to meet. This was not one of those times. We believed that an individual had information that would allow us to identify someone who we suspected was planning an attack. We did not believe that this individual knew the person we were looking for; rather, they had the intel we needed because of their role and access to information at their company. If this seems vague, I apologize, but it's all I can reveal. For the purposes of the story, what you need to know is that this was an urgent matter that absolutely could not wait, and the person we were looking for should have been willing to help us—we weren't asking them about their brother or anything like that.

It was wintertime but it wasn't particularly cold out so my temporary partner that night and I weren't bundled up in bulky coats and hats. We were just two plain looking early-thirties white guys in suits and black winter coats. We probably looked more like insurance salesmen—not people you were super excited to speak to but hopefully you were not afraid of either.

It was a nice suburban detached house on the corner of a T-intersection of a busy street. A large fence wrapped around the front of the house, shielding it from the traffic of the main thoroughfare. The driveway was located to the side of the house and accessible from the quieter street. It wasn't late but it was already dark when we arrived. The first thing we noticed was that we couldn't get to the front door. There was a freshly plowed driveway, but the large gate at the side of the house that led to the front door was locked. It was clear that the residents used the garage to go in and out of their house. We peeked over the locked gate and could see that the snow had not been shovelled on what we believed was the path to the front door. There were lights on in the house. We ran around to the busier street and saw a woman moving inside.

We didn't want to draw too much attention to ourselves. This person was not suspected to be in any way involved in any threat-related activities, so we didn't want to alarm his family or neighbours. We discreetly tried to wave to try to get the attention of the woman. It didn't work. We went around to the garage and knocked on the garage door. We waited. No answer. We went to the other side of the house that was accessible. It looked like a mud room or laundry room. We could hear a washing machine and dryer humming inside. We knocked on the window. Nothing. We knocked louder, assuming she couldn't hear us over the laundry machine. Nothing.

We couldn't leave. It would be one thing if the house was completely dark and we didn't think anyone was home. Even then, we'd have probably gotten in our car and waited. In a way that would have been better. We could have caught someone coming home and engaged them before they got through the garage and into their fortress. That wasn't the case. We could see there were people in the house, they just weren't answering us.

We went back to the gate and had a discussion about legalities. This was the first time I'd actually worked with this partner. I think if we had been more familiar with each other we might have egged each other on and gotten into trouble. As it was, we fumbled around proposing things but nothing too outrageous. The gate was locked but the lock was a latch that had a string attached to it that could pull it up. The string was on the other side of the fence and we couldn't reach it. We tried to see if we could wedge our fingers through to lift the lock. We looked for sticks or other utensils we could fashion that might do the job. Nothing. Perhaps if we'd had more time or more tools, but we didn't. And we debated. Should we just jump the fence? Is that legal? Did our job that night supersede the law? If my co-worker had said confidently that we should do it, I might have gone along. I suspect if I'd said the same thing he might have as well. Neither one of us was very confident in our legal footing, so we went back to what we knew. Knock louder. Gesticulate wider. Do our best MacGyver impression on that stupid lock and fence. And that's when the cops showed up.

Three cruisers rolled down the quiet residential street. Mercifully there were no sirens and no lights, but clearly they were coming our way. The neighbours noticed too. A few lights came on at the homes across the street. The only questions at this point were who had called them and what were we going to say. We were honest. We had our badges out, and we showed them to the first officer who approached us and the other five who joined our impromptu huddle in the driveway. We told them who we were and broad strokes about why we were there. We apologized for the disturbance and bringing them all out.

At that moment the garage door slowly opened. It was dark outside; the garage was fully lit, and standing there at the edge of the driveway was a very small, slightly terrified middle-aged man in a mismatched sweatsuit. If he was happy to see the police, he wasn't happy long. The lead officer walked right up to that man and kind of berated him. He told him he needed to speak with us and tell us what we wanted to know. He barely introduced us or explained that we were CSIS. I thought he could have been a little gentler. It was almost like the homeowner was in trouble. He invited us in apologetically. My partner and I felt bad for the guy.

To make matters worse, when we stepped inside we were introduced to the man's wife and ten-year-old son. My heart really sank thinking of how terrified they must have been that they'd called the police rather than just shooed us off on their own. We recovered, though. His wife made us some tea (it had got cold out there after a while), and the gentleman went to his office to see if he could find what we needed. Once he understood who we were and that he wasn't in trouble, everything worked out.

There isn't one interview I haven't looked back on and wished I had done things differently. There are questions I didn't ask or things I said I wished I hadn't. It happens every time.

I honestly can't remember much from the conversation that night. But I do thank God we didn't jump that fence. Certainly, that would have made for a different interaction and conversation with the cops.

In the end we did get the information we needed from the individual. From that we were able to isolate the source of the threat, and that helped us determine that it was not a direct threat to life but more likely internet chatter that did not and would not materialize. It was a relief, obviously. In this case the individual was extremely helpful. Even if there wasn't a threat, to be able to rule it out and not suck up more resources chasing it down was a win.

Having the police there to vouch for us helped. That time it was the homeowner who called the cops on us. One time I actually needed to call the police on myself. People know what the police are. Maybe they couldn't tell you what Toronto Police Service detachment number jurisdiction they live in, but they generally understand what the police do. CSIS not as much. I would say ninety-nine percent of cold call conversations I've had with people go this way:

ME: "Hello, my name is Andrew. I'm here from the Canadian Security Intelligence Service and I need your help."

INDIVIDUAL: (*Blank stare*) "What?"

ME: "I'm from the government. CSIS."

INDIVIDUAL: (*Faint recognition*) "Oh, police?"

ME: "Actually, CSIS is established under the CSIS Act . . . Section 12 mandates us to investigate four main threats to the security of Canada . . . Those threats are terrorism, espionage and sabotage, foreign-influenced activities and subversion . . ."

I appreciate that it can be a lot. If you don't know what CSIS is and you have some people in suits standing on your front steps telling you they come from the government and want to ask you questions about your friends, co-workers and neighbours, I don't blame you if you're skeptical. I am also sensitive to the fact that many new Canadians come from societies where their domestic intelligence service can threaten, harass and otherwise frighten their own people. The Arabic term for intelligence service is Mukhābarāt. Of course, that has a much more negative connotation in some Middle Eastern countries. Sometimes if I could see that my CSIS introduction wasn't registering, I'd simply say, "Canadian Mukhābarāt. Nice Mukhābarāt." That might get a laugh and a foot in the door.

Even people who know what CSIS is might not believe that the people at their door or on the phone are from CSIS. Could you tell the difference between a real and a fake CSIS badge?

Most of the time, for the willing but skeptical participant, I'd tell them to go on their phone or computer and look up the number for CSIS themselves, or I'd offer to get them the public number. Then I would give them my name (which was the alias I used). I told them to call the CSIS number and tell reception that they'd met me, and then to leave a code word or message for me. The person on the other end of the phone would not confirm or deny that I worked there but said they would pass along the message. I would get the message and tell the person the code word. I hoped that would satisfy them that I was who I said I was and worked where I said I worked. If in the process they learned a little more about CSIS by googling us, all the better.

On one occasion, however, this did not satisfy an individual. I was working in Windsor with a female colleague. We were both dressed in business casual attire. We weren't wearing dark suits, but we certainly looked professional. The contact wasn't satisfied by our normal vetting process. She asked for additional confirmation that we were who we said we were. She wanted to talk to the police. Ordinarily we might not do so, but it was important, and we were asking this lady for some sensitive information. We called in a favour at the local police department. We asked if they could send someone over to have a word with the woman to assure her we were legitimate.

Our buddy showed up; he was clearly on his day off. He was a bit of a mess—he was wearing shorts and a mustard-stained golf shirt. I think he'd literally walked off a golf course. He walked by us on the front steps and knocked on the door. The lady answered, he flashed his badge, she said okay and that was that. I don't think he gave his name or his badge number, and he may or may not have had a gun on his hip, but that would have been it. I mean, could you tell the difference between a real police badge and a fake one any better than a CSIS badge? Well, it was enough for this woman.

My partner at the time was pretty annoyed. I was just so jealous. Every conversation, it was such a pain in the ass to explain what CSIS was and what we did and why they should help us. This cop just walked up to the house and all those questions were answered. I felt like I was trying to meet a girl in college and had spent all night trying to impress her, and this guy shows up with his mustard-stained shirt, flashes a badge and gets her phone number. Now maybe she would have eventually fallen for me too, but there was such a disparity in the level of effort it took to get credibility. Until that time, all I knew was my frustration trying to explain what CSIS was. Seeing up close the level of authority people place in the police versus all the work I had to do . . . that really stung.

You Get Out What You Put In

My community interviews and tracking down of piecemeal intelligence from the Americans continued for about a year. We reestablished our network of contacts and engaged the community to assess the threat information we received. A few of the leads did come through with some substantial intelligence. We found a couple of people with significant ties to Al Qaeda in Iraq. They were very cooperative and willing to share information on some of their contacts back home that were engaged in threat-related activities. Those were big wins.

Eventually the community engagement front started to quiet down, though. The leads stopped coming from the Americans and we did not have any threat-related activities to track down at home. Once again, the priorities on the desk started to shift as they had before. My desk got a shake-up as some IOs were transferred and I was handed another file that would involve fewer welcoming chats over tea.

Wouldn't you know it, though, a few years later I got a phone call from one of the community contacts. It was now 2014 or 2015 and the war in Syria was raging. Iraq was back in the news because of ISIS and there was a growing concern that people from Canada and other countries were going to Syria to fight.

The call came from someone I hadn't spoken to in a couple of years. He was a contact dating back to those original 2005 cold calls from my predecessor on the desk. A community member had sought out his help. They were concerned because they had overheard a group of kids talking about going to Syria to join ISIS. They turned to this respected member of the community, who then relayed that information to us. It was no longer my file, so I introduced him to an IO who was responsible for the newly established foreign fighters desk. My colleague got the relevant information, and his team was able to investigate. Long story short, the threat was resolved. All from a friendly tip from a community leader with a relationship of trust developed over years.

One of the reasons I wanted to write this book is to explain this part of the job to Canadians. It isn't the dangerous or sensationalized spy work you see in the movies. In fact, most of the spy movie references we have are from government agents fighting terrorists in far-off lands or a romanticized version of recruiting diplomats at foreign embassies. One of the unique features of our domestic intelligence service is that this is all happening at home. I was having coffees and conversations across the city where I lived, picking up pieces of information here and there and building relationships so that members of the public would feel comfortable letting me know if something was wrong. The threats I was investigating were local, and the pitch was to work with me to help keep us all safe. Most of the time this all went very well and there was no reason for anyone to ever hear about it. It's only the bad interactions that make the news.

The Credibility Chasm

On that note, the CBC reported in August 2019 that a couple of people set up a student support hotline at the University of Toronto's Institute of Islamic Studies, in partnership with the Canadian Muslim Lawyers Association and the National Council of Canadian Muslims, because they were concerned about visits they'd received from CSIS and wanted to advise others of their rights before speaking with the Service. That they felt the need to do so made me sad, but the CSIS reaction actually made me angry. It was a boilerplate emailed response: "[CSIS] builds relationships with individuals to collect information and advise our government about threats to national security... When CSIS seeks cooperation or assistance from Canadians, we emphasize that discussions are voluntary..."

First of all, there was such great irony in the whole situation. The fact that these young people were approached and then set up a whole organization with the cooperation of other major groups just demonstrated to me that they are *exactly* the type of people CSIS should be reaching out to. What a missed opportunity!

Let me be clear on this point. I understand that getting a call or visit from your domestic intelligence service can be nerve-racking and may make people feel uncomfortable. These meetings are also in some ways like first dates with the intelligence officer. You can have bad chemistry and not want to see the person again. Even though people are under no obligation to speak with CSIS, it is still a core part of CSIS's mandate to reach out.

That's what makes it so frustrating that the bad experiences are the only ones you ever hear about. When situations like this occur, where groups feel targeted and CSIS's intentions are questioned, instead of shrinking I'd like to see the organization take the opportunity to raise its profile and publicly defend its mandate. A canned, impersonal and passive response to public concerns (warranted or not) will do nothing to help to build trust and confidence within the communities they serve.

The organization's limited public engagement can't help but fuel skewed media coverage, leading to distrust and contributing to the negative view of CSIS. I've seen the corrosive effect that has on the Service's reputation. In 2014 I was sitting at home in Toronto watching TV and I got a call from my brother. He started asking me about Mohamed Harkat, who was arrested in 2002 under a security certificate and accused of being a threat to national security. The government had ordered Harkat deported. He had run out of legal appeals so he was making an emotional one. It was a very unusual call. My brother never asked me about national security or what I did. To paraphrase our conversation, he said, "I know you can't talk about what you do. But I'm sitting here watching the CBC and they are interviewing this guy Harkat and his wife and they're crying, and I feel bad. Should I feel bad?"

What I said was, effectively, "You know I can't talk about specific cases or reveal any evidence that may or may not have been used in this case. What I can say is that the Supreme Court of Canada upheld the security certificate. You do not have to believe me or him. You can listen to the Supreme Court."

What else could I say? Not much. It hurt that I had to convince my own brother that CSIS wasn't some malicious organization picking on random people. I wish I could have introduced him to the very real and dedicated intelligence officers who'd spent years of their life on that file. But you don't get to hear from them. You do get to see Harkat on television.

This isn't just an issue for the public. The CSIS mandate is to collect and analyze information and intelligence on threats to the security of Canada and advise the government. CSIS's limited profile, and more broadly the organization's reluctance to share information, is going to lead to a credibility problem with its stakeholders too.

As a public example, in 2010, the CBC reported CSIS director Richard Fadden saying that some members of municipal governments and two provincial cabinet ministers had possibly come under the influence of foreign governments. The director came under a tremendous amount of pressure, and it seemed there was a possibility he would be forced to resign.

Years later, it was widely reported that in 2010 CSIS had actually briefed the Ontario provincial government and raised the matter directly, saying that an Ontario Liberal minister was "susceptible to interference" due to his close ties with a foreign government. The government of the day got a review from the Office of the Integrity Commissioner, an office with a totally separate mandate and powers than CSIS, and relying on this secondary review dismissed the allegations. To add insult to injury, this incident was eventually made public and CSIS was denounced in the news for "McCarthyism."

In this case, I give CSIS some credit for at least taking a risk and informing the government of concerns. However, they must also share the blame that those warnings were so totally dismissed. CSIS is notoriously tight lipped. The Service is always delicately balancing the requirement to inform government against the risk of that sensitive information being disseminated wider than intended. This is a longstanding existential crisis. An old colleague of mine used to say to any senior CSIS executive who would listen, "What's the point of having all this great intelligence if we don't share it with the people who need to hear it?"

I don't know the extent of the threat and I wasn't in that room for the briefing. But from what I read in the news, the national security intelligence agency responsible for investigating threats to Canada had a confidential briefing with the government, and that wasn't enough to get them to take any measures to mitigate the risk. Maybe CSIS wasn't saying enough, or maybe the government didn't take the warning seriously. Either way, it's a problem.

I fear in this era of "fake news" the confidence people have in our institutions is waning. I worry about an erosion of support from people who in the past would have been willing to assist CSIS. But more than that, I fear the severe consequences for our country if that lack of confidence leads us to tune out CSIS's warnings. Just as important as people continuing to help when asked, when CSIS says there's a problem, even more need to listen.

Hooking Up, Getting Serious and Coming Clean—In No Particular Order

Working in the regional office was much different than my time in Ottawa. For starters everyone at headquarters was kind of stuck there. Geographically it was in a pretty remote location so there weren't a lot of places to physically go to socialize nearby. Then there was the nature of the analyst role. I spent pretty much all day in front of the computer, so I had little to no reason or excuse to actually leave the office. After-work gatherings just didn't happen all that often. It was a government town with public-servant hours. Most people drove to work. They punched in, punched out and headed home, farther into the suburbs where they lived.

By contrast, the Toronto office was downtown. A lot of younger intelligence officers lived in shoebox condos that weren't very far away (myself included). The nature of the regional investigator job also meant we were constantly coming and going. It wasn't a nine-to-five, core hours job. When I was an analyst, I supported operations. I would show up at the office and work would come to me. As an investigator I was responsible for my own schedule. I was expected to take the initiative to track down leads and work my files. I'd have my meetings, which could be during the day or in the evening, then I'd have to write the reports and do additional paperwork like expenses and file-update memos. At the same time, I'd be sent information on my cases from foreign partners or headquarters as well as conduct my own research into new leads and figure out who to connect with next. No two days in the field were the same, unlike in Ottawa, where every day for two years was exactly the same.

I'd generally sit down on Monday morning and try to figure out my week: who I was going to call on the phone to schedule a meeting, who I was going to try to surprise at home, where they all lived and when I would carve out some time for the follow-up paperwork. While I was based in downtown Toronto, a lot of the people I was meeting with were not. CSIS has its own fleet of vehicles that we had access to for our investigations. I'd take into account traffic when plotting out my days, avoiding the gridlock of getting in and out of the city at rush hour as much as I could.

For most of us, Friday was paperwork day. It was also usually a casual day, which led to a relaxed and social atmosphere around the office. Bullpens could be pretty empty during the week and then full of IOs on a Friday. It would be an opportunity to catch up, and it wasn't uncommon on a late afternoon to have a drink in the office or go for one in a bar nearby. There were still a lot of commuters, but if we chose a pub between the office and the train station, we'd generally get a pretty good crowd out for at least one drink.

I loved my downtown Toronto field agent lifestyle. I walked to work in the morning and took full advantage of the flexibility that the role demanded. If I had to work late one night, I'd come in a little later the next day. If I started to feel claustrophobic behind my desk writing a report, I'd grab a company car and go knock on some doors. I always kept a few people and addresses to check in my back pocket, ones that weren't a priority but a good excuse to get up and go. We were given almost total freedom and expected to be out of the office, having meetings and collecting information. If we were seen around the office too much, some supervisors would come and shoo us away.

I was also now a single man in my hometown. I went back to online dating and found the issue of my job and meeting women was totally different than in the nation's capital. In Toronto I said I worked for the government and eyes just glazed right over. Either people didn't care or, worse, they thought a little less of me. Especially when I tried my best to make it sound boring and change the subject. It is amazing the different impression of public servants in Toronto versus Ottawa. In Ottawa everyone wanted to know my level so they could figure out how I'd got there. In Toronto, people wanted to know what had happened in my banking career and why I'd ended up in government.

The anonymity of working for the government was helpful, but I was also very conflicted. I was a spy. It was a cool job and would probably make me more attractive to women. I also knew I wasn't supposed to tell people. And what's more, I never wanted to use my job to get girls. I was constantly debating what the appropriate order was: Do I tell them I'm a spy before things get serious? How serious does the relationship need to be to tell them I'm a spy before it gets awkward when I do?

The lying really didn't feel good. I remember I was dating a girl and she wanted to get together one evening. I told her I wasn't feeling well and was just going to be taking it easy that night. She offered to come by and drop off some soup. It was very sweet but of course

I had to say no. I wasn't actually at home; I was in a hotel room in Scarborough getting ready for a meeting. I'm not really sure what she thought. Either I was a jerk or I had other plans I didn't want to tell her about. I know I didn't feel great about it. I wasn't sick, but I totally would have had the soup.

I actually ran into a familiar face from my previous Toronto online dating experience when I stumbled across the Jewish girl from Montreal on a different site. It had been five years since our ill-fated date. I thought we'd had a nice time, other than my obvious bad timing on the kiss front, so I decided, Why not? I played it cool, pretending I didn't recognize her. I sent her a pretty standard email hello. I think I included something to the effect of, "I'm online to meet people I wouldn't normally meet." She wrote me back, "I'm pretty sure we went on a date five years ago?" I was busted. I wrote her back, "Yes, of course ... I remember. I think we had a nice time." She replied, "Who can remember. It was so long ago." Her responses were a little harsh, but she did keep writing me back, so I took that as ... not a good sign, but still an open door. I asked her if she wanted to grab another drink, and she said yes.

We were back at Carens, the wine bar in Yorkville. It was our second first date and three out of three dates at the same place. Looking back, I'm not sure why I didn't suggest another place. It might have even been garbage night again. It went much better this time. I actually found out it wasn't the kiss that had turned her off but the fact that I was in the army. At the time I'd been just starting out my reservist career. Back then I'd been on Facebook and had put as my profile picture a photo of me in uniform holding a c7 rifle. She hadn't been into that and had ghosted me.

I think this time around lying about being a spy actually helped me. Working late and being unavailable played to my advantage. One evening during our courtship, she and I were making plans to meet up at the CJPAC Action Party. This is an annual massive gathering of politically engaged citizens and socially active single Jews. She was going with some friends and I was going to stop by later on. My interview that night went long and I didn't end up going to the event. I texted her later and said I wasn't going to make it.

Ordinarily I would have never made and cancelled plans with someone. In fact, I would have gone out of my way to be there. I would never have just not shown up. This was a very uncharacteristic "bad boy" move. And you know what? She admitted later that she thought I was playing hard to get and it definitely got her a little more interested. All those times I had to brush women off because I needed to work late and all the seemingly phony excuses I made to get out of doing things were out of character and definitely not my natural dating style, but it actually kind of helped.

Despite (or maybe because of?) my unintentional game playing, we got serious pretty quickly. We were both at the age and stage to know what we were looking for. I was feeling good about my career and settled now that I was back in Toronto. I was putting down roots and looking for a partner to do that with. I was also comforted by the fact that I had met her before I'd joined CSIS and was reasonably confident she wasn't a foreign agent.

I was getting ready to tell her I was a spy when she actually dropped a big reveal on me first. On our fourth date she told me that the main reason she'd gone out with me a second time (this time) was because of a bet. As you can tell from our first date five years prior and our email exchanges kicking off this round, she could be a little tough on guys. She had never suffered fools, and she wasn't meeting anyone she liked. Her friends thought she needed to increase the number of guys she met, so they made it a ten-date challenge: she had to go on ten dates in two months. If she did that, her friends would take her out for a steak dinner, and if she didn't, she'd have to pay for the meal. When she saw me pop up online, her first thought was, Well, this guy wasn't terrible, so that's an easy date to get my numbers up. Her second thought was, It's been five years so he can't still be in the army. Joke was on her! I was still in the army reserves, but at that point I was deep in my career at CSIS so well off Facebook.

On that same date I told her I was a spy.

I leaned in over the table and seriously but quietly told her, "While I work for the government, I don't write policy. I am actually an intelligence officer with CSIS." She paused for a second and looked at me. I almost felt like I was knocking on a door. Like a reflex, when I saw her expression I was about to go into my routine: "The Canadian Security Intelligence Service is our domestic intelligence service..." She stopped me. "I know what CSIS is."

She didn't treat it like it was a big deal. I think she thought it was cool. Or at least, she was happy I was being honest about it. While she might have known what it was, she probably didn't realize in that moment what it would mean for our relationship. She found out quickly. I asked her if she would please not tell a lot of people. For whatever reason I made up an arbitrary number and said she could tell one person. I assumed she would want to tell someone, so to say "Don't tell anyone" wasn't realistic or fair. She said she'd tell her sister.

A few days later we went on a double date with her best friend. I knew right away her friend knew. She actively avoided asking me any questions about work. I was used to parrying questions, so when I didn't receive any it was noticeable. We got in the car after the date and I said, "You told her I'm a spy, didn't you? I'm not mad, I just would like to know." She admitted she had. She'd told her two best friends. I understood. I should have asked her who she wanted to tell, not given her a random number.

The fact is, I did want to contain the number of people who knew but I was becoming less dogmatic about it. I was no longer worried about some deep undercover operation that was never going to come. I especially didn't want to do a silly song and dance, lying to someone's face when they already knew where I worked. If her friend had asked me what I did, and I started going on and on about policy work for the government when she knew I worked for CSIS, I would have felt like an ass. At work I had been advised to be discreet. As I got more experience as an IO, I became more comfortable using that discretion and cautiously widening the circle of people who knew.

We made our own deal: if there was someone she felt she needed or wanted to tell, I asked her to just let me know first so we could talk about it. I thought that was fair. I was no longer keeping this secret myself but asking her to lie for me. I tried to convince her to wait a bit to tell her parents. Like my indiscreet contact showing off my business card, I worried they were so proud of their daughter and happy for our relationship they might promise discretion but not be able to keep it. We didn't keep them in the dark for long, though. We moved in together after three months and I started looking for a ring. At that point we both felt it was only fair that they knew their future son-in-law was a spy.

7

MY GUY

CANADA IS one of the safest countries in the world. This is not because we don't face threats, but because we do an admirable job of protecting our citizens against them. That is how law enforcement and intelligence agencies tend to work. If we do our job, you won't know we were ever needed in the first place.

Every once in a while, our successes make the news, such as the foiled Toronto 18 plot in 2006, wherein a group of homegrown radicalized Canadians wanted to detonate truck bombs in crowded locations in southern Ontario. More recently, in 2016, Aaron Driver was confronted by the RCMP in his driveway in Strathroy, Ontario. He was believed to be on his way to carry out a suicide attack. He detonated the device he was carrying in the back of a taxi, wounding himself and the driver, and was then taken down by the RCMP before he could inflict more significant damage.

We aren't perfect, though. In 2014, Michael Zehaf-Bibeau shot and killed Corporal Nathan Cirillo, a soldier who was standing guard at the National War Memorial. Zehaf-Bibeau then stormed Parliament Hill but was killed before he could reach the country's leadership. This attack was devastating, not only cutting down a Canadian soldier but threatening the heart and head of our government. Our national feeling of safety and security was truly tested. For a time. Then our collective memory faded, and we once again went about our lives not worrying about terrorism and believing it was something that didn't happen here.

The public complacency is understandable. However, this comes from the luxury of evaluating national security within the narrow parameters of what happens exclusively in our own backyard. At CSIS, the landscape was global and the threats never stopped. It is believed Zehaf-Bibeau himself had plans to fight in Syria. Apparently, he'd applied for a passport but it was delayed, and the frustration of being unable to leave the country may have been a motive for him to carry out his attack at home.

During my time at CSIS, many of our successes and failures received less attention and generated less concern because they happened or would have happened overseas. The following is not an exhaustive list that has been publicly reported in the news. This may seem like more cases than I need to support my point. However, the reason I want to include a number of examples is to emphasize this: just because Canada was spared from a large-scale domestic attack does not mean that Canadians did not carry out atrocities and horrendous acts of terror around the world in this "age of terrorism."

Tamim Chowdhury, from Windsor, Ontario, left Canada in 2013 for Syria to fight with the Islamist State. He became a leader in the movement and was believed to have been the architect of the July 2016 Dhaka café massacre that killed twenty-nine people.

André Poulin was from Timmins, Ontario. He left for Syria in 2012 and was featured in an ISIS recruiting video. It's believed he died in August 2013 during an attack on a government-controlled airport.

Salman Ashrafi, from Calgary, Alberta, left Canada in 2012 to join ISIS. He reportedly blew himself up a year later in a suicide mission in Iraq that killed forty-six people.

Damian Clairmont took on the moniker Abu Talha al-Kanadi ("The Canadian") after he left Calgary in 2012 to fight for ISIS in Syria. He was killed by the Free Syrian Army in Aleppo in 2014.

Ali Medlej and Xris Katsiroubas went to high school in London, Ontario. It is believed they left the country around 2010 and travelled to Morocco, Mauritania and eventually Mali to train with Al Qaeda–linked Algerian terrorists. In 2013 they were a part of an attack on a gas plant near In Amenas, Algeria, that killed at least thirty-seven workers from eight different countries. It is believed they died in the attack.

Mahad Ali Dhore was a student at York University. In 2009, he travelled to Somalia to join the Islamist group Al Shabab. He was also featured in a recruitment video, and in 2013 he reportedly died during an attack on the Supreme Court of Somalia that killed more than thirty-five people.

Fawzi Ayoub, who lived in Toronto, was reportedly a commander in Hezbollah, a designated terrorist organization by Public Safety Canada. He was arrested in Israel in 2002 while attempting to organize a bombing attack. He was released in 2004 when he was traded to Lebanon in a prisoner swap. In 2009 he was indicted by the United States for another attempted bombing in Israel and then placed on the FBI's "Most Wanted Terrorists" list. In 2014 he was reported to have been killed while fighting in Syria on the side of the Assad government.

Hassan El Hajj Hassan, who lived in Vancouver, was convicted in absentia for his involvement in a suicide bomb attack on a bus full of Israeli tourists in Burgas, Bulgaria, in July 2012. The bus driver and five Israelis were killed, with more than thirty-five other Israelis injured.

Most recently, in 2019, Patrik Mathews, a former Canadian Armed Forces reservist from Beausejour, Manitoba, and suspected member and recruiter for a neo-Nazi paramilitary group called "The Base," disappeared and was suspected of fleeing to the United States. He was later apprehended. Although strikingly different ideologically, operationally The Base models itself after Al Qaeda. For starters, Al Qaeda translates to "the base" in Arabic. They also both send foreign fighters to geopolitical conflicts around the world with the aim to return more effective fighters, ahead of a race/religious war they hope to launch in North America.

There are unfortunately many more examples. By April 2019, Global News reported that Canadian terrorists had killed and injured more than three hundred people in other countries since 2012. I'm sure that's much higher now. Canadians have also been victims in these and other attacks around the world. Of the 2,973 victims on 9/11, twenty-four were Canadian.

CSIS has a responsibility to protect against threats at home and, as a member of the international community, a duty to ensure our country is doing all we can to prevent attacks that might be carried out by our citizens in foreign countries. This was a concern we had about someone I was about to become very familiar with.

My time investigating threats from Al Qaeda ended with a shake-up on my desk. Some senior IOs were transferred, and it was determined that I would take over as the primary intelligence officer on an investigation into an individual who was deemed to be a threat to national security. He had been a target of investigation for a few years, and the threat was deemed significant enough that a federal court judge had approved a CSIS application for a warrant that authorized additional intrusive investigation and collection techniques. I would be responsible for managing the file. It was known that he had sympathies with the ISIS terrorist organizations and the concern was that he might either conduct an attack in Canada or go overseas to undertake operations abroad (become a "foreign fighter"). I would work closely with other people on my team as well as our counterparts at headquarters, who assisted us while overseeing the national program. However, as the regional investigator, this individual was ultimately my responsibility. He was my target, "my guy."

The investigation had been going on for a few years. My target was young (early twenties) and we believed he was being radicalized online by a friend abroad. Their conversations had been picked up by a foreign intelligence service, and we were made aware of our local connection to this wider network. By the time I got involved in the investigation the online recruiter had been arrested and their relationship effectively severed. They certainly were no longer talking openly about conducting operations or travelling abroad together to join the fight.

We needed to understand how radicalized the young man had become. Did he still have plans to travel abroad? What was the likelihood he would conduct an operation at home? Would the arrest of his recruiter (or facilitator) give him pause or harden his commitment to jihad? He had a tight circle, and when I took over he had become much more discreet in his conversations and suspicious of those around him. He was well aware that his friend had been arrested and was certainly alert to the possibility that he was on someone's radar too.

In my previous role my mandate to engage the community was broad, but now I had a singular focus. I inherited human sources who reported on my target, as well as technical sources such as the electronic intercepts on his phone and computer that monitored him. It would be my responsibility to manage these human and technical assets and lobby my management for more resources (surveillance, support officers) if they were required to fill intelligence gaps on the file.

There is a lot of horse-trading in managing a file. I would make my case to my supervisor and he would lobby his superiors until ultimately the senior management would decide who got what. The resources weren't unlimited, and decisions were made on a daily basis. Things had a way of changing quickly too. The surveillance coverage on targets was booked in advance. Things came up all the time we hadn't known about when the schedule was originally decided. It was pretty common that I would find out last minute that my guy was planning on doing something I'd want to know about, like meeting a new contact, on a day I didn't have surveillance. I'd then have to track down the investigator whose target had the coverage I wanted and ask for a swap.

As the lead investigator on my file, I became the point person for this loose system of resource brokering in offices and hallways. Sometimes the trades could get complicated and occasionally senior management had to arbitrate. I always tried to be reasonable in my requests so that when I really needed something, I would have a stronger case. It was a challenging file and a real threat. It was also not unlike many of the threats we were triaging in the Toronto region at the time.

Eyes on the Prize from a Comfortable Distance

The surveillance teams are not made up of intelligence officers but specially trained individuals who work together to covertly follow and observe a person of interest. A major misconception perpetuated by the Hollywood depiction of spies is that one individual can track another person for an extended period of time or distance on their own. There have been a few movies where someone picked up their target at an airport and then, all by themselves, managed to follow them to their hotel or house without being seen. Impossible. It takes a full team working together to stay close enough to track someone's movements, but far enough back to avoid detection.

It is extremely difficult to do it well and it takes many trained surveillants to follow just one person. Sometimes I'll read a story in the news about a politician or commentator wondering why we don't have 24/7 surveillance on all of our targets. Well, it's just not feasible. On top of the fact that you need a number of people to follow one guy, part of the job of a surveillance team is to identify unknown associates that come in contact with the target. An active team may have to split to undertake a few different sub-assignments during the same general surveillance job. These folks don't work twenty-four hours straight either. They can't. There are multiple shifts covering multiple people that have to overlap at some point to smoothly transition. Factor in Toronto traffic and our subway system, and the demands of the job are unbelievably complex.

After I took over the case, I made it a point to go out on a few ride-alongs with surveillance teams that were monitoring my guy. I had read up on the file, but it was important for me to get an understanding of what he did day to day; to see the places he visited and how he interacted with his friends and associates, not just read about it in the reports.

Some of his associates were human sources. Did they look as close as the sources assured me they were? I wanted to understand whether things he did looked natural, or if he was practising any operational security or counter-surveillance. I know the surveillants appreciated it when the 10s came out. It showed them that we were invested and interested in their work. It allowed them to ask questions of us as well. They didn't have access to all the information on a file so they would ask us if things made sense or if there were individuals we were aware of or weren't. In many cases they would get closer to the target than I ever could, and they would have invaluable information to fill in blanks in our investigation.

Despite our different roles, we were a team and it made us better when we were working together. They were also a limited resource. Like I said, there wasn't a lot of surveillance to go around. When it was my turn, I wanted to make sure we got as much out of it as we could.

I didn't have the patience or ability to be a surveillant myself. They could spend hours at a time watching a front door waiting for someone to come out of it. It required a focus and a visual acuity that I didn't have. They needed to be far enough away not to be seen but also close enough to be able to recognize and separate their target from anyone else they might be with. Some were definitely better than others at the spotting part. And they knew who they were. Other surveillants were notorious for their inability to pick out their target from a crowd at distance. "I got him. He's heading your way." Then minutes later you'd hear the next surveillant say, "Not our guy. Not even close. Our guy is a six-foot-four white guy. This guy is maybe five eight and Asian." There was always good-natured ribbing. It reminded me of my military unit with the inside jokes and teasing. I did love the camaraderie that I got to see in small doses.

Spying Is the Friends We Made along the Way

After getting to spend some time following the target (at a safe distance), it was time to meet the people who were close to him. Since I had inherited a file that had been going on for a while, I also inherited the human sources who had been reporting on it.

It is said that someone does not really become a source until they've been handed over from their original recruiter. That speaks to the principle that a confidential informant does not work for the person who recruited them but for the organization. It was also an unavoidable fact of life in the regions because of the high turnover of IOs on investigations.

In theory it makes sense, but it could be hard in practice. There is often a very strong bond between a recruiter and their source. To get someone to provide information is a big step that is often facilitated by a tight interpersonal relationship built on trust and developed over time. Even sources who have been handed over many times can get annoyed with a change—especially when they like the person they've been talking to.

On this file, I had the unfortunate privilege of taking over some sources who had been meeting with a very attractive, smart and fun female IO. They got along great and it was an incredibly tough act to follow. It was an unintentional bait and switch. They were fine to continue to meet with me, but I had no doubt where I ranked in their preferences. I had worked on human source policy and administration for years. I knew everything you were supposed to know about how to recruit, manage, hand off and even end a human source operation. There was nothing in the book about taking over a source who had a bit of a broken heart.

I have to be very delicate here about what I say as I don't want to give away source handling methods or any information that could be used to identify people that I met with or who worked with CSIS. Of course, I've changed some details of my stories to protect those involved. But there is one story I'd like to share because it demonstrates a bit of the relationship that we have with our human sources and what it was like to be out from behind the human source operational support desk actually dealing with the people rather than the policies.

You can get pretty close with the people you meet. We send sources into the community to collect information and then we are there for them to debrief, vent to and confide in after they do. In many ways we are their most intimate confidant. The setting can also help. Meeting someone in a coffee shop or over lunch is pretty relaxed. With sources we would often meet in hotel rooms. We could order room service and, if they drank, even have a couple of beers. It was work but it was more private and familiar. This was important to maintaining the secrecy of the meeting but also really did help forge closer bonds.

I was meeting with a source who was a devout white Muslim convert. We did not share beers but rather bonded over talk of spirituality and relationships. He loved giving me dating and marriage advice from the Quran. We had one unfortunate meeting on Ramadan and a particularly hot summer day. He was an observant guy so he was not eating or drinking. It was late in the afternoon and he was really struggling. We were trying to strategize how we would deal with a challenging situation. This was made more complicated by the fact that he was having a hard time getting words out and was feeling light-headed. I was really worried about him.

It only got worse. He got up and went to the bathroom. He said he was going to try to put some water on the back of his neck. He was in there for a while. I didn't want to check in case he was drinking and didn't want me to see. I knew he was stressed, and obviously part of that stress was working with me. I tried to give him a little space to collect his thoughts. More time passed. I called out and he said he was okay. The door didn't open. I started to get very concerned for him, and for me. I ran through scenarios. What if he passed out? What if he passed out and hit his head? What would I do? He wasn't a large guy, but neither was I. Worst-case scenario I could drag him down a hallway and into a car. That would be terrible operational security and wouldn't be great for CSIS's reputation if anyone saw it. I texted my supervisor. Should I force-feed him food and water? Could I expense the candy from the mini-bar? What was the paper-work required to admit someone to a hospital? Would I sign that using my real name?

Mercifully he re-emerged and we got through the meeting. I got the information I needed and he was able to somewhat collect himself. I wanted to drive him home or send him in a cab, but there was no way. How would he explain that or come back and get his car later? I cared about him and felt terrible to see him this way. He had gone through great pains to be there when he clearly wasn't up for it. He assured me he was all right to drive home.

I thought back to my time on the human source policy desk. It put some of those battles I used to have with the regional investigators in perspective. They would be advocating for their sources and I would be enforcing the strict letter of the policy. I wondered if I would have been as tough if I'd had source-handling experience doing that job and seen first-hand what some of these sources go through to help and some of the unique situations you find yourself in together.

The people I met and worked with could not have been more different and each of them worked with me for their own reasons. For some it was loyalty to Canada; for others there was the financial incentive. It wasn't always altruistic. Nevertheless, almost all went above and beyond what I asked of them. Most were Muslims and they were working for the Canadian government in a time of particularly elevated anti-Muslim bigotry. They struggled to find work and knew that society looked at them as terrorists when in fact they were anything but. I wish I could point them all out and give them the personal acknowledgement and public thanks they deserve.

I've met a lot of police officers and I know that it can be incredibly challenging, emotionally, to constantly be dealing with some of society's worst representatives. Investigating those who are acting out their worst instincts and seeing the horrors that people can do to each other must be soul destroying. My work at CSIS was very different. The people I met with regularly were absolutely characters in their own right, for sure. They had a variety of quirks and idiosyncrasies. But they were inspiring, not deflating. We were a team and they gave me everything they had—even if I knew, deep down, that they all preferred the attractive, smart and fun 10 who came before me.

It was around this time my career in the army came to an end. I was working during the day and into the evenings meeting with sources while also trying to find time to spend with my fiancée. My weekends became much more precious personal (and couple) time, and it was a bigger sacrifice to spend them in the woods on a military exercise. I was also the main investigator on my target. There was a risk if I was unreachable. Canadian Forces bases are notorious for their poor cell reception, and I hadn't told anyone in the army that I was in CSIS or that I needed any special accommodation.

One weekend I was on a firing range on the base taking part in a machine gun qualification shoot as part of a larger support weapons course I had been taking. There were some developments on my file that we were tracking closely, and management had taken an interest. I had some concerns about going away but I knew I would have access to my phone, and I got special permission to drive my own vehicle to the base in case I needed to leave "for work."

I got a text requesting an update from the second in command of the Toronto regional office while waiting to shoot. I ducked behind the ammo vehicle for some cover from the noise to make the call. It wasn't very effective but it was the best I had. I forgot the second in command didn't know about my military career. She was caught off guard in the middle of our chat when bursts of heavy machine gun fire started rattling off in the not-so-far distance.

"You okay? Where the fuck are you?" she asked, confused and slightly concerned. I apologized and tried to explain as I found better cover to finish the call.

The issues never materialized, and the call came from my own office, not a source, which was fortunate. It was a bit of a wake-up call though. I'd enjoyed my time in the reserves, but realistically I was past the point of preparing to go to war. However, I *was* responsible at home for an important national security investigation, and it was an expectation of my role that I would be available 24/7 if needed.

Not So Incognito

As I briefly mentioned, there are different threat levels and designations for subjects of investigations, which determined the authorization for additional resources that could be used. You couldn't just use every investigative tool in the organizational toolbox on anyone. I used to joke that to raise money for the Government of Canada Workplace Charitable Campaign, CSIS should auction off surveillance for a day on a person of the bidder's choosing. It wouldn't be allowed, of course, because there were rules about who we were and were not allowed to follow. They had to meet a threshold of a threat—it couldn't just be for a good cause.

As a case developed, the investigator would have to provide a rationale as to why they needed additional powers and what specific gaps of information we believed those powers would help us collect. The aim was to balance the intrusiveness of our actions with the threat posed by the individual. The highest or most intrusive powers were "warranted." That meant an application had been made to a court for a judge to authorize the violation of the individual's right to privacy such as it was necessary to carry out the CSIS mandate. My target was warranted so I had every tool at my disposal.

So in addition to the physical surveillance and human source reporting, I was also authorized to technically intercept the target's communication. By the time I took over the file we were already electronically monitoring his phone and email to help us get a better idea of what he was doing and who he was communicating with. It was now my job to ensure that these were the target's methods of communication (that we weren't intercepting someone else's) and that we weren't missing anything. Back in the office, I also had to make sure I had the resources to actually listen to them.

Technology is great and it's possible to intercept and record a lot of things. However, everything we collected still had to be reviewed and assessed. It's one thing if you miss something—the person was talking on a burner phone you didn't know about or using a pay phone you couldn't intercept—but it would be something else entirely if you had a phone call on tape but didn't review it in time or missed the significance of it.

I don't envy the translators and communications analysts for that. They have to wade through all the calls, emails and internet searches of all the monitored targets to make sure they are alert to the smallest clue or indication of threat-related activity. Many of them have been with CSIS for decades. They are from every ethnic and cultural background. Some of them are grandparents. Every day these analysts come to work to review the communications and computer-viewing habits of the highest priority targets of national security investigations. They sit in front of multiple big computer screens, put on their large noise-cancelling headsets and end up watching a lot of truly horrible pornography. It's actually pretty disturbing. In the security clearance interviews I conducted I didn't hear anyone admit to watching the kind of stuff these guys were watching. I'd try not to look at the screen if I was coming into their office. Occasionally, one of their earphones would come unplugged and you'd hear the audio. It was an unfortunately gross part of the job, but everything had to be reviewed.

I regularly went to check in with the analyst who was reviewing my target's communications. It was important to stay engaged with her. She was listening to conversations and reading his emails. She knew him the best. I would read the reports and she would reach out if something big came up, of course. Still, there were things that were better discussed in person than read off a page. She knew when he was having family problems or money issues, and she knew all the neighbourhood gossip that might not be threat-related intelligence, so wouldn't be included in a report, but could paint a picture of the target's state of mind and whether circumstances in his life were making him more or less prone to acting out.

My target lived with his parents, and in this conversation with the analyst it became increasingly clear to both of us he was using his parents' computer. Obviously, it was important to know what he was looking at. Was he buying plane tickets? Using some messaging app we didn't know about? It was a concerning information gap in our investigation. I told her I was going to request an intercept on the computer. I was hopeful we might find something. She was just expecting more porn.

Getting additional communication analyst resources was a challenge. I wasn't trading surveillance with other investigators—once the technical collection started we couldn't let days go by with no coverage. I made my request to management, then went to pay my respects to the supervisor of the communications unit. This was less a negotiation than its own recruitment. She managed her team, and her support would be critical to free up resources that could be deployed on my file. There is absolutely a triaging and prioritization of investigations at CSIS. Personal relationships matter too. Respectfully advocating and lobbying for internal resources was as much a part of my role as lead investigator as recruiting sources.

The communications supervisor had been around a long time. She had an open door and was easy to talk to but careful about committing her analysts before putting you through your paces. She would start with a smile as she warmly advised, "I just don't have the resources." She would then ask me what desk I was on and who else we were asking her to monitor. She wanted to make sure I was on top of my file. How many lines did I have running? How much activity had there been? Just as she wanted to protect her people, I think she also wanted to make sure things were fair across the other operational desks. I explained why it was important, and she said she could move some things around to accommodate my request but we would need to review in a few months. She always found a way.

After a few weeks we got my computer intercept up and running and started to receive the target's intercepted traffic. I wish I could say this is where we found the smoking gun and blew the investigation wide open. It wasn't to be. It was simply more porn. The communications analysts really do know their targets best.

Next Time Please Just Send a Postcard

Warrants provide the authority for our most intrusive investigative powers, but there are checks and balances in place to ensure that we are following the letter and the spirit. It's like that CD I knew I shouldn't keep during my role-playing exercise in training. Just because someone is a target of investigation doesn't mean there is carte blanche. In the course of my investigation, I ran into the limits of my powers. Although in this instance, unlike in training, initially I "took the CD."

It came to light that another target (tangentially related to mine) who was currently overseas had kept a Canadian mailing address in Toronto. He was out of the country but was still having mail delivered to his ex-girlfriend. We thought this was a promising lead and something worth investigating. As it was related to my guy, I was tasked with tracking it down. Then things got complicated.

Mail is very sensitive. You cannot just open someone's mail. I knew this. My hope was to see generally what the mail was and where it was from. You can tell a lot from an envelope. Is it a bank statement? Telecom bill? Is there a phone number you don't know about? I called up his ex to arrange a meeting. She was happy to help. He'd been gone for years and they weren't on good terms. She brought up the fact that she had been receiving his mail, which was great. I didn't have to reveal I already knew that.

I went and knocked on her door, and we had a nice conversation. Eventually I got around to asking about the mail. "Could I see it?" I asked. She said, "Sure, you can see the whole thing. I've opened it already." *Shit*, I thought to myself. "You didn't open it because I asked about it, did you?" In my mind I knew that would be a huge problem. No, she said, her ex had asked her to open his mail. Apparently he was waiting for something and he wanted her to let him know when it arrived. Great, I thought. The person whose mail it is has asked the person who lives at the address to open it. Then it has to be okay for that person to tell me what's in it. In my estimation they no longer had an expectation of privacy. But I'm not a lawyer. And that's why we have lawyers.

If you remember, there was a large discussion in training about the CD my role player slipped into my bag at the mall. Was I allowed to have it? Did I need to give it back? Well, now the question was, Did I have the right to this person's mail? It was open, but was I allowed to look at it? I got back to the office with some notes on the contents of the mail. It was by no means critical information but it provided some background on the individual and really just confirmed some dates related to when we believed he had left. There wasn't a lot there and certainly not a lot of threat-related information to report.

That didn't stop the lawyers from getting involved. I didn't try to hide anything. I honestly didn't care either way. I thought I was right. If I was wrong, I was willing to accept that and throw myself at the mercy of a review. I wasn't trying to break the law. In my mind, once the subject of investigation gave permission for someone else to open their mail, that person had the right to show me what was in it. Would it have been different if they had told me and not shown me? I didn't think so.

I believe the legal argument came down to the fact that the subject of interest only gave the other person permission and not me. Really? I thought. What if there had been a smoking gun? (By the way, there is never a smoking gun.) Would I not have been able to report it? I had my opinion, but it wasn't my place to make the final decision. These conversations about the letter, spirit and nuances of our authorities happened all the time. I let the reviewers and lawyers sort it out. As someone who had been on the other side, I respected the process even if I didn't always agree with the outcomes. I assume someone back at headquarters had to write a memo.

Never Meet Your Heroes

My day-to-day work life was consumed by my target. He was young and religious, with a labourer job. He followed events happening overseas extremely closely and engaged in animated discussions with his friends about the Egyptian elections in 2012 and growing civil war in Syria. He saw the events happening in the world and wanted to be a part of them. A part of me could relate. After all, I had joined the army following the events of 7/7. Was he going to do the same thing on the other side? For me, every day was dedicated to finding the answer to that fundamental question.

He had been a target for a few years, so by that point our investigation was a pretty well-oiled machine. I was getting a steady diet of quality information from our human sources about what he was saying in public and confirmation from surveillance and my communications analyst on what he was doing (and revealing) when he thought nobody was watching or listening. There wasn't much daylight between the two. It was the same chatter that had been going on for a while: a lot of talk and no concrete action or indication he was planning on doing anything about it. This wasn't unusual. For many targets, the investigation can continue in a steady state for years. Alternatively, threat-related activity can intensify and it can also go dormant. Very few investigations lead to formal RCMP charges.

I was in regular contact with all my stakeholders: my supervisor, communications analyst, headquarters support and senior management. We were in agreement that it might be time to wind down the investigation. My target was sucking up a lot of resources and it was getting tougher to justify it over some of the other investigations with more active and threatening targets. Before we did that, though, my boss suggested I try to talk with him. To sit down face to face with my guy, personally evaluate him and make a final determination if I thought he was a threat. It would also be an opportunity to try to softly recruit him. To see if he was open to speaking with us. He had excellent credentials given his past comments and ties to an overseas terror recruitment network. It would be a real coup to turn him.

One of the arguments for meeting my target was that our great human source and technical coverage of him would probably mean we would get insightful feedback from the approach. His reaction would be informative in assessing him. Would a call or visit from CSIS anger him and expose a higher level of threat than we thought was there? If he kept it quiet that would also speak volumes and perhaps suggest he was open to recruitment.

Meetings like this were always revealing—and sometimes comically so. A female colleague once interviewed the friend of a target of her investigation. She was hoping he would keep the conversation quiet, but we found out that two minutes after she left the interview, the person called the target, and we caught it on tape. He said CSIS had come to talk to him and that he'd told them to fuck off and that there was no problem, et cetera. My colleague was disappointed that her conversation had made its way back to the target.

She was heartened moments later. The target asked the interview subject who it was from CSIS that had knocked on his door. And the guy said, "Some skinny blonde bitch." My colleague's face lit right back up.

"Did you hear that?" she asked the room. "He called me skinny!"

She dined out on that one for years. We joked that the next time she got a haircut she should go back to the guy and see if he noticed, and then we could listen to the phones and hear what he really thought.

I was excited about the opportunity to meet my target. It didn't happen often. As I've explained, investigations can last a long time and intelligence officers are constantly moving on and off desks. This isn't like a human source. There aren't formal hand-offs. You certainly wouldn't call a target up to introduce yourself and say that you are the person in charge of the investigation against them. There's an obvious advantage if the person you're investigating doesn't know they're being investigated.

There also has to be a clear rationale to meet. CSIS's mandate is to collect, analyze and retain information and report to government on threats to Canada. We didn't have threat reduction, mitigation or disruption powers at that time. The CSIS Act was very passive. For example, I couldn't say to the target, "We are on to you. Stop what you are doing." Nevertheless, a visit from CSIS with frank questions with a direct tenor, tone and line of questioning could convey its own message. If that seems like splitting hairs, I'm inclined to agree.

As a side note, this changed later with Bill C-51, which provided CSIS with additional powers to take more invasive actions (with a corresponding approval process). The bill was brought in at the tail end of my time so I don't have much insight into how it played out in practice, and would once again refer anyone interested to pundits much more qualified than I to comment on the academic and legal pluses and minuses of it.

Getting back to my target, in the case of my meeting with him, our objectives were probably a little of column A and a little of column B. He had been met before but not for a while. We thought he might be curious who the new guy was. Maybe we would have a better rapport than the previous investigator he'd met? Ideally I could solicit threat-related information from him and recruit him to provide more. We were hopeful but also hyperconscious of the fact that the exercise could backfire.

Meeting a target has to be approved at the highest levels because the final consideration is safety. Targets by the nature of their designation have been identified as a threat to national security. By meeting them, CSIS is knowingly potentially putting an IO in harm's way. This wasn't a casual door knock. There were additional security precautions that would have to be taken. The entire surveillance team would be deployed to follow him before and after the meeting and to keep eyes on me inside. They wanted to make sure he showed up alone and did not appear agitated. They definitely wanted to make sure he didn't try to follow me or confront me during or after the meeting. The communications analyst was on call to make sure I wasn't going to be ambushed or surprised in any way. Getting the support and approvals for this meeting took all my horse-trading, cajoling and persuading powers. It would be a collective team effort and took weeks to arrange. Finally, the plan was in place.

To make the call I used a phone in an empty boardroom down the hall from my bullpen in the CSIS Toronto office. I wanted the privacy. I was also feeling a lot of pressure. I had made all of these arrangements based on the assumption that I could get him to agree to a meeting. If he said no, I'd have to report to the most senior levels of my office that I hadn't got it done.

I was alone in the boardroom. I shook out my limbs and literally jumped up and down a few times to get some nerves out of my system. I dialed the number and felt myself shaking a bit as it rang. I managed to keep my voice steady when he picked up the phone. I said, "Hello, my name is Andrew and I'm calling from the Canadian Security Intelligence Service. I think you may have information that would assist me in a national security investigation. I was hoping we could meet for coffee at your convenience to talk." I paused and waited for his response. He agreed.

Up Close and Personal

We arranged to meet at a little diner close to his house. I got there extremely early to make sure I got a quiet seat in an ideal location. I could have had breakfast and lunch in the time I had before our meeting. I wanted to be able to see the front door and have a rear exit behind me. I also wanted to give myself lots of time to get settled, to gather my thoughts and communicate with the surveillants who were tracking his movements prior to our scheduled time.

I was honestly expecting typical jokes and chirping like, "He's loading his gun" and "He looks pissed." To my mild surprise, the surveillance team played it straight. They gave me a detailed run-down. I don't want to say they weren't always professional; it was just that in that moment, the absence of the typical lighthearted banter in the face of my looming target showdown was a little unnerving.

I wasn't worried about him attacking me, but you never know. Also, I wasn't armed with anything. Nobody at CSIS carries weapons. I was fine with that. I was a member of the army and well trained in weapons handling and safety precautions. I still wouldn't have felt comfortable bringing a gun to a meeting.

The surveillants advised that he was making his way to me. I did a final scenario run-through of what I would do if things went bad and how I would alert them if I needed help. I was ready.

My target arrived at the diner. He took a moment to have a cigarette in the parking lot, then stepped inside to look around for me. We had never met before, but it didn't take long for him to figure out who I was. I was sitting alone wearing a blue button-down shirt and blue blazer, with my brown hair parted neatly to the side. I hadn't tried to look like a typical agent; that's just my general aesthetic. I thought it appropriate to be professional but not stuffy. He had come straight from his construction job. He was wearing work boots with dusty jeans and a faded dark T-shirt. He was a little more dishevelled than I was, after a long day working in the hot sun.

He sat down in the booth and I motioned for the server to bring him a coffee. After she dropped it off, I showed my badge and started in with my standard introduction about the CSIS mandate. I didn't mention that I knew he'd previously met with a colleague and he didn't bring it up.

We did a quick casual recap of the weather and traffic. It was strange to be sitting across from the guy. I knew everything about him: his background, what he liked to do in his spare time, his family, his friends, who he was honest with and who he wasn't. I had seen pictures of him: some formal, like his driver's licence photo, and others that were grainy surveillance pictures taken with bad lighting and weird angles. He was slightly bigger than I imagined. And although he was young and fit, he was not imposing or intimidating in real life. He slouched in his chair on a slight angle and avoided making extended eye contact.

After initial pleasantries I started into more personal but still very general questions. Where was he from? What did he do for a living? Did he like it? I was hyperconscious not to indicate how much I knew about him or reveal any information that would raise suspicion. We were covering very light ground—his life in Toronto and his feelings about Canada. As I got more comfortable, I asked him some direct questions I knew the answers to, to see if he would be honest with me. He was. He was also coy about things I knew he'd be coy about—namely his close associates in Toronto and friends abroad.

Sitting across from him I could really take the measure of the man. Read his expressions when he answered questions. Consider his thoughtfulness and receptiveness to my rapport-building attempts. As the meeting went on, I could see him relaxing a bit. He might have thought I was going to come in harder with more pointed questions. When those didn't come, his guard came down ever so slightly.

I took the opening to move the conversation to international events, specifically in the Middle East. His body stiffened only slightly as he sat up, turned and engaged directly with me. He was now reading me too. To see where this was going. I could feel him look me up and down.

I dug deeper into how he felt watching events unfold abroad while living in Canada: his loyalty to his adopted country, how he felt about Canada's foreign policy and feelings about the broader Middle East. I would never expect him to say he hated Canada, but his views on foreign conflict would also be informative. I asked him specifically about the war in Syria. What did he think of it all? What were his views on ISIS and the Assad regime?

He had made his assessment of me and decided he wasn't going to hold back. He opened up, noting his particular disdain for the Shia Muslims in Syria and around the world. It might surprise some to know that many Sunni Muslim extremists despise Shia Muslims. It was a rant I had heard from him many times in the reporting from his conversations with friends. Now it was coming directly from him. He was still angry, but somehow it was less threatening hearing it in person. And then he stopped. And he rolled back into his seat and he stroked his big bushy beard and said, "You know, Andrew, they are worse than the Jews."

I don't think I've ever felt more Jewish than in that moment.

It caught me by surprise. I'm not sure why. It's not like I wasn't aware of anti-Semitism or the widespread hatred of Jews. I had even heard comments on the job. Mostly they were off-hand remarks or wild conspiracy theories shared in coffee shops by people I'm sure didn't know I was Jewish but probably should have known better. The Jews created Al Qaeda. Israel controls America through special interest groups or the media. There were no Jews in Palestine originally. Israel knew about 9/11 but didn't tell anyone. The people who made these claims weren't looking for a debate, merely conferring upon me their knowledge of world events.

I took a moment to consider my response. He was reclined but I felt his eyes were still on me. His comment was really apropos of nothing and I couldn't tell if he was messing with me a little bit. I don't think he thought I was Jewish, and we certainly hadn't talked to that point much about Israel. He assumed that either I agreed that Jews were awful, or it was just universally accepted that Jews were awful so to really hammer home his disgust with Shia Muslims he'd used that benchmark. He could have been trying to get a rise out of me or testing to see if I would push back. Bottom line, I was still trying to build rapport and I wasn't there to try to change his mind. So I leaned back in my chair, stroked my naked chin and said, "Wow, that bad, eh?"

He looked at me and solemnly nodded in the affirmative to confirm his indictment. It was a strange but very real bonding moment.

As we said goodbye, I asked if he would be open to meeting again. I thought we'd had a productive conversation. I told him that I could learn a lot from him. I appreciated his knowledge of current events, and CSIS was very interested in his view on what was happening around the world. It was all true. I didn't want to give him a hard sell, but I did imply that I valued his time and insight. We'd only had the coffee, and I suggested that perhaps I could buy him lunch next time. He said he was interested, but it never materialized. It seemed once he met me, he was less inclined to meet me again. Over the next few weeks I would call him up and try to get him out for that lunch. He would say yes and then cancel at the last minute. Finally, he said flat out he didn't want to talk to me anymore.

He didn't mention our conversation to anyone. It didn't appear to make him angry or scared. He just kept it to himself like he was trying to put the whole thing behind him and forget about it. In fact, his conversations with friends even softened. He didn't want to meet with CSIS, but I do think we left an impression.

Saying Goodbye and Hopefully Not See You Soon

I apologize if this is repetitive, but I feel I need to say it again: there are people in Canada who are a serious security concern. These are bad people who want to do bad things either here at home or abroad. My target of investigation was believed to be one of them. We didn't put these thoughts in his head or words in his mouth. They were there and my job was to determine if he was going to act on them. This was the age of terrorism. He wasn't alone. The Toronto 18 plot was a legitimate, homegrown terror group that was trying to blow up buildings and kill a lot of people. The Via Rail terror plot involved a couple of guys who wanted to derail a passenger train. This isn't just my opinion, either—the ringleaders were convicted in a court of law of serious criminal offences.

For my guy, the question wasn't whether he *wanted* to do something, because he repeated in private and public conversations that he did. We had to determine: Will he? And if so, what, where and when would he do it?

Intelligence files aren't like law enforcement cases. CSIS isn't reacting to a crime and then building a case to arrest someone for it. An individual may be investigated and assessed as a threat under the mandate and never meet the threshold for formal charges. Theoretically, an investigation could go on indefinitely. There are rules for a minimum requirement for investigation, but once someone crosses that they get added to a list of ongoing subjects of national security concern. CSIS doesn't declare them guilty or innocent of a crime, it constantly evaluates the threat, triaging and prioritizing each investigation with decisions made daily over limited resources.

Ultimately, I came to the conclusion that my guy was not an ongoing risk to engage in threat-related activities. Like many people online or in the comfort of their living room among friends, he was a lot of talk. Perhaps if the arrested terrorist recruiter had stayed in his life he may have been moved further along from his speeches to deeds. But at that point he had been saying the same thing for years, and our conversation did not change our evolved hypothesis that he was not likely to take action. I bounced this conclusion off my boss, my HQ counterpart, my communications analyst and other people involved in the case. We all agreed.

I then started winding things down. We stopped monitoring the target's communication. Over time I handed over my human sources to other investigators who could use them on their cases. Eventually I became the last resource to go. I was transferred to another file on the same desk. At first, I would still indirectly hear about my guy. I'd get informal updates from the intelligence officers my new sources were working with. They would still see my old target from time to time. Finally I got moved to a different unit and the updates stopped.

It's a tough thing to close a file. A lot of people had worked on it and names are not chosen at random. My target had been involved in terrorist planning and there were many reasons to suspect that he could again. In the back of my mind, I worried about him. If he did do anything, I felt it would be on me. At the beginning there were nights I really worried about it, but as time went on, it was less.

I can get triggered, though. When I see mass atrocities committed by individuals, especially if we learn that they were at one point on the radar, I run through a series of emotions. I first get very angry at the attackers and perpetrators of the crime. I am incredibly sad for the victims and the many lives ruined by the senseless acts. And then I am brought back to the conversations I had at work: the haggling in the hallways over surveillance coverage, the stop-ins with my communications analyst and the long debriefs with my supervisor where we would try to make sense of the target's actions to assess his state of mind. These are the same conversations that the other intelligence agencies must have also had. Did my counterpart miss something? Were they screaming from the rooftops that they needed more resources but their superiors made other decisions? Or maybe the file was closed and down the road this individual took a horrible turn. I don't know. The task of getting it right on every individual, on every decision, every single day, is impossible.

When there is a terror attack like Paris, San Bernardino, Orlando or Berlin, I am glued to my screen. Like most people, I want to know more about what happened. But for me, more importantly, I need to know who did it. Even though it's in another part of the world I always think of my guy again and get a terrible sinking feeling in my stomach. I watch the news very closely. I put on CNN and I scroll Twitter. I need to hear the name of the attacker and make sure it wasn't him.

Are You with the Bride or the Spy?

My wife and I got married in Toronto in March 2013. We had a very small Jewish ceremony before sundown on Friday night with immediate family and then a much larger not-quite-totally-kosher ceremony with a party on the following Saturday night. I was born and raised in Toronto, while my wife's family is from all over: Montreal, New York, Florida and Peru. The crowd was a mix of family and friends from many different groups. There were high school friends, university friends and past and current work friends. A good crew from CSIS came to the wedding. It would be the first time my wife and family would meet anyone I worked with. I was definitely a little nervous about it.

I didn't have a set cover story for what I did and I had no idea what the broken telephone description of my job was that had made it through our extended families. I think one of her cousins thought I was a mailman. I know her aunt thought I installed security cameras. Nobody had bothered to correct her because they didn't know any more than that. Now there was going to be a whole table full of people who "worked for the government" with me.

I didn't gather my work colleagues and give them a proper advance brief about what I told my family I did for a living. There wasn't much to say besides "generic government job and have fun with it." It was a song and dance we all did so I trusted them to handle it. That didn't mean in the back of my mind, with alcohol and the celebratory atmosphere, a part of me didn't think the cat would surely get out of the bag in some way or other.

My fears of being fully outed as a spy were probably overblown, and the reality of the situation was I was in no position to police it or do anything about it. I was so busy dancing, partying and not eating

I barely had a chance to see what everyone else was up to and who was talking to whom. At one point in the evening, though, I did see my brother and my supervisor talking. They were both over by the bar, drinks in hand, in what looked like a very deep conversation. Or rather, my boss was doing the talking and my brother was doing some intense listening. My brother noticed me staring and gave me a look of pride that seemed overly reverent, even considering the occasion of my wedding. I had to get closer to listen.

I wandered over towards the bar, not trying to interrupt them but definitely trying to hear the conversation. I wasn't as stealthy as I had hoped, and they broke off their discussion. Before they did, I heard my boss blurt out, "And that was the third time I put my life in your brother's hands..."

To this day I have no idea what they were talking about. Both my boss and my brother claim the details of their conversation got lost to the evening. The truth was, at that point I don't think I could count three times when my life was ever in danger. Let alone when I was rescuing or protecting my supervisor. It was clearly an embellishment, but I wasn't going to argue about it. Heck, I don't know if my brother has looked at me the same way since.

I'm sorry if this book burst that bubble. Up to that point in my career, I had been a productive intelligence officer. The nature of my files meant that while I had a few tense moments and incidents that could have escalated, my work in the field did not consistently rate on the danger scale. That was soon to change. We had a ten-day honeymoon in Mexico planned, and I'd be coming back to a new team and a new assignment. My next post was in special operations. Things were about to get a lot more exciting.

8

BACK OF THE VAN

THE SPECIAL operations security team is the elite group that executes warranted powers. As I've mentioned, warrants give CSIS additional authorization to use intrusive investigative techniques, such as listening to phones or searching private property to further an investigation. It isn't the violation that is sanctioned but the right to access certain privileged or private information. However, having the right to access information and actually getting it are two different things. You could go up to the person and ask them for their phone, but then you would be telling them that they are the subject of a national security investigation. Instead, the regional desk investigator (my previous post) will make a request to the special operations team to procure that information covertly.

My old target was warranted. There were a lot of people involved in the warrant application and termination process, from regional investigators, headquarters analysts and senior managers who are the sworn applicants to the lawyers who submit the request to the court. The invocation of those powers, however, takes place in the region and involves a special unit trained specifically for these clandestine operations.

I first met the special ops team when I had a request for assistance with my target. I had reason to believe he was hiding threat-related information at his work and I knew when we would have a window of opportunity to get access to it. I went to the supervisor of the unit to float the idea. He was initially keen and asked me what day I had in mind. It was Halloween. He had been working non-stop for months on a very high-profile case. He let out a deep sigh and said, "Buddy, I haven't been home on Halloween for a few years. You got any other days for this?"

I didn't have another day at the moment, but I told him I'd get back to him with a few options. I could tell he didn't want to say no, and I didn't want to force him to say yes. I know he appreciated it. The supervisors on the operational support desks held a lot of sway. It wasn't worth pushing on this one. There would be other opportunities, and some leeway on the timing might get me some goodwill. It did.

We got another opening, and to show his appreciation for my flexibility the supervisor asked if I wanted to come along on the job. This typically didn't happen. I'm not sure if it was even allowed, but I got to do a special operations ride-along. I sat in the back of a car and listened over the radio as the team broke into the office, then found, collected, copied and replaced the information I was after. I heard it all unfold in real time while the supervisor who was driving the van narrated what they were doing and why, like a director's commentary. This was *Mission: Impossible* stuff. I was hooked.

Much like the *Mission: Impossible* crew, the special operations team is made up of an eclectic cast of characters, each with their own unique skill set. The remote-access specialists are men and women who are experts at accessing information through a variety of cyber/hacking methods. The close-access specialists are adept at getting their physical hands on the information or devices we are looking to target in operations. Their specialty is finding, moving, copying and returning something back to its place without anyone noticing it's been touched. They can also hide things where nobody will find them. There is one guy who is simply responsible for locks. He's called "Locks." That is all he does—open locks. The makeup of any one special operation depends on the skills required to accomplish the mission.

As an aside, Locks practises all day opening, or "defeating," locks. He has his own practice kit, which he's beaten so many times it's no longer a challenge. It's basically four locks drilled into a horizonal wooden board. Each lock gets increasingly more difficult. There are lock picking tools he uses, and he lets intelligence officers practise picking the locks for fun. I was never able to get even the easiest lock open. I tried a bunch of times. I just didn't have the touch. I brought the board back to him and watched as he completed all four locks in about ten seconds while carrying on a conversation with me about where we were going to go for lunch. His only challenger that I remember came at the CSIS Toronto office grade nine take-your-kid-to-work day. (Yes, CSIS has a take-your-kid-to-work day—probably the first day many young teens find out what Mom or Dad really does for a living.) One year a kid showed up who picked all four locks in a matter of minutes. He claimed he had never done it before. He was a locks savant. We were all in awe, and I think Locks got a little nervous too.

Supporting these specialists are intelligence officers like me, called the special operations security team. Their job is to create and execute a plan to get these technical specialists in place to conduct the operation. Get them in, out and home. Consider a race-car pit crew. Each member of the crew has a specific job that they do in seconds to get that car in, serviced and back on the road. Now imagine that race car is parked in a parking lot or a driveway. The pit crew's job doesn't change. If the mission was to plant a listening device in a car, then the specialist's job was to choose the device, find a place in the car where it could work and plant the device in the car. The security team's job was to get the specialist to the car, give them enough time to do their job and then get them back from the car without them or the device getting detected.

The technical specialists stay in their roles for the duration of their career. The intelligence officers rotate in and out of the team. Special operations, however, are by their nature complex and dangerous. There are limited spots and they only take fully trained and high-performing intelligence officers into the unit. It is an elite team doing very cool work. I wanted in, and through a combination of luck and good timing, when the next spot opened up, I found myself selected to be on it.

We Won't Fuck with You—Life Will

The new job would require specialized training. There are techniques and methodologies to planning and conducting a special operation. There's a course designed to teach us and let us practise in a controlled environment. It had been about six years since my initial intelligence officer training in Ottawa. I was now returning to the same classroom at CSIS HQ for a much different learning experience. It would be three intense weeks in Ottawa that brought together new special operations security and technicians from regions across the country. We all lived out of a motel working 24/7. During the day we would be in classrooms or in the field getting practical training. At night we'd scout the areas we wanted to conduct the operations in. We'd try to find some time before or after class to write our operational plans, get some sleep and then conduct the operations. The long hours and relentless pace of the course were intentional. It was designed to see how we'd perform low on sleep and stressed out to the maximum. They wanted to push us and re-create the stress of the job. The obstacles would appear on their own.

I remember the first briefing we had. The trainers were all current members of special operations teams with years of experience. The lead trainer was a grizzled veteran of hundreds of jobs. He stood before us on the first day and told us, matter-of-factly, "We will not be fucking with you guys on this course." He continued, "We will not be creating any arbitrary or artificial obstacles, tricks, traps, nothing. Real life has a way of getting in the way. When that happens, we don't want you to think that we did it. We trust things will get fucked up on their own without us."

I remember that speech clearly because it didn't take long for him to be proven right. It happened on our very first training attempt at a covert entry into a condo unit. There were two teams working that night. Our team had made it into the unit okay. The second team got delayed. We could hear some commotion on the radio. We didn't realize what had happened until we left the building. Just like us they had parked in the rear parking lot behind the building. There was a small paved path from the parking lot to the front door. It was maybe four metres long. It wasn't wide enough for two people, so I guess rather than go single file one of the other team members had decided to approach the building on the surrounding grass, and wouldn't you know it, he happened to step in a huge pile of dog shit. You could not have done that on purpose if you'd tried. If he'd stepped a couple of inches in either direction, he would have missed it. He didn't. He stepped right in it.

I saw some of the aftereffects when I was leaving the building. There was dog shit smeared everywhere. He had tried to wipe it off on the path outside and even on the stairs inside the building. It was a total and complete mess. Plus, it stank, and that really was the problem that wiping couldn't solve. He smelled like shit, and you can't bring that smell into someone's house, and certainly not when you don't want them to know you were there.

It was a good first lesson in special operations. It's the advice I give to people when I give a talk about security. Be alert, communicate and have a plan. When that plan changes, make a new plan. In this case we had made a very detailed operational plan for the training exercise. We knew the order of people going in, what everyone's job was supposed to be, how long it was supposed to take, et cetera. What we didn't plan for was that smell. So in that situation, when the plan changes, you stop, communicate and make a new plan. They went back to the van, did a quick shoe change with the guy driving and continued. It wasn't a huge setback, but it was a lesson I will always remember. It probably left an impression on the guy stuck in the van with the shoe as well.

The biggest thing we learned we could not control was pets. I'm not a fan of cats, mostly because I am allergic to them. My eyes water, my throat tightens and I sneeze—a lot. Sneezing is not a positive on a clandestine special operation when nobody is supposed to be where you are. I quickly learned that my "go bag" (all the things I would carry with me on an operation) needed to include allergy medicine. We also learned that our operational plans would need to account for cats or other pets because they were such a wild card. We did a job on a house, and as soon as we opened the front door, the cat just ran right outside into the street. It was like he knew we were coming and was waiting to mess with us. Mercifully this happened during a practice exercise and our trainers took pity on us. They said to continue with the training mission and one of them would go out and try to round up the cat. If it had happened on a real job, the whole operation would have had to stop until we were able to get Kitty back home.

The course as a whole was gruelling and a lesson in humility. The pace and the expectations were much higher than in my original intelligence officer training course. Instead of bringing in donuts, we would start our morning debriefs getting berated by our instructors for the mistakes we'd made. It was consistent with the stakes of the job. Special operations were the most sensitive and dangerous tasks CSIS undertook. A failed job could end up on the cover of the *Globe and Mail* and cause an international incident or, worse, get somebody hurt. Things happened, and there were a lot of ways to screw up: forget tools behind, leave marks on furniture, install equipment that doesn't work, make too much noise. We did it all. That was the point: to learn those lessons in a controlled environment and understand how they could affect an operation.

At times it felt like we were playing a game, breaking into houses and learning how to steal cars. I'd have to catch myself occasionally and remind myself that it was real. The places we were going into and cars we were taking were loaned to us for this purpose, but the neighbours weren't told what was going on. I knew teams had been caught and police called on previous courses.

At one point during this training, I remember being in a condo, crawling on my hands and knees under a window, with a flashlight in my mouth, trying to keep myself and the light out of view of anyone who might be watching from outside. I had always felt a part of CSIS and proud of my contribution to the important national security work we did. But in that moment, I really felt like a *spy*. It was exciting and exhausting, cool and terrifying, all at the same time. It was exactly what I'd signed up for when I'd submitted my CSIS application all those years before.

The course ended and I returned to the unit fully trained but the most junior member of the team. Special operations largely works on seniority. You start out in a support role and you slowly get more experience and additional responsibility for planning and leading missions.

I was a little disappointed to learn we didn't have our own individual code names. After having so much fun naming sources, I was excited to get one myself. Instead we used call sign numbers on each job that signified role and seniority. Number One was the team lead. Two was second in command and often assisted with planning the operation. Three, Four and Five held subordinate and supplementary roles as required. Typically, the lowest number was the driver. This was the safest spot to be and the least likely to encounter the public during an operation. In the rear with the gear, as we'd say in the army.

I apprenticed for a while under my more experienced co-workers. In the field we looked out for each other. The team needed to know they could trust you with that responsibility. I started in the back of the van. They didn't even let me drive at first. That's where I began to learn the ins and outs of the job. I would see the plan unfold and hear over the radio how the team communicated and worked together to accomplish the mission. The next level up would be deploying to an area to be a lookout or relay information. The leads would be the ones escorting the technical specialists to the most sensitive areas. I tried to soak up as much as I could, anxious and excited to move up the ladder.

Live Your Cover

It wasn't long until I learned the value of a slow apprenticeship and the fact that even in the van things happen in the real world that training can't prepare you for.

That first lesson was how to live your cover and hold your nerve. As most people are aware, a "cover" is a story that is created to conceal or obscure our true identity or the real reason we are doing something. When I was meeting with sources in hotel rooms, I would have a scenario in mind that would explain my presence if I was ever approached by someone I knew (or didn't know) about why I was there. This would change depending on the location, time and other details of the meeting. The goal of the cover story was to present a plausible explanation that would conceal the true nature of my activity.

One of my first tasks with special operations was to survey a neighbourhood. I wasn't expected to get out of the car. I was just going to do a drive-by at night with a partner to get a look around. Was the street dark? Were people awake? Was there street parking? I was to gather this information and feed it back to the team lead who was putting a plan together.

It was late, maybe 2 a.m. We were parked on the street and were both sitting in the back seat of a four-door car with tinted windows. It was easier to sit in the back for taking notes. To anyone looking out their window we would have looked like a parked car. I could throw a jacket over my head to cover up any light I might need. I didn't plan to be there long. Ideally at that time of night there wouldn't be much activity on the street, and if we needed to we could get out of the car, walk around and get a sense of things. Were there motion sensor lights? Would dogs bark if you walked past a house? It was important to know these things and feel comfortable walking around a neighbourhood if you were going to plan an operation there.

I never got that far. We were still in the car when we saw someone. My partner noticed him first. A random guy had walked out from a house down the street. He didn't have a dog and he wasn't smoking. Those were the two main reasons for anyone being out at that hour. Another one was if a social gathering or party had broken up and people were leaving the house. This guy seemed to be all alone.

At that point we had a decision to make. Do I climb into the front of the car and drive off? Or do we hang tight and let him walk by us? We looked down the street and didn't see any cars near us. We quickly tried to figure out where he was going. Would he be getting into a car and driving off? There were a few cars parked behind us, between the guy and us. If he did get into a car, it would be before he got to us. It didn't look like that was where he was headed, though. He wasn't walking close to the sidewalk. He was in the middle of the street. He must live close, we thought. Maybe he was hooking up with someone and heading home. We hung tight.

Special operations is a constant test in living your cover. Once you construct the story or rationale, you have to commit to it fully. You have to be comfortable operating within that made-up scenario when people are around you. It can feel very strange. The aim is to convince others that it makes sense. And it only looks weird if you make it look weird. You simply cannot bail out anytime someone is close by. You need to be able to keep your head, believe in your story and carry on. In this case that meant to sit tight and let the situation blow over. Moving attracts the most attention. At that time of night, it might have looked strange or even alarming to that person if he saw us suddenly scramble to get into the front seat and drive off as soon as he approached. In this scenario we were sitting in an empty parked car. We had our cover story. We hoped it would hold.

We locked the doors and crouched way down in the back, our heads low in the seat so we weren't giving away a silhouette. We held our breath and froze, waiting patiently and still for him to pass by. The last thing I said to my partner was, "Not one word." We couldn't turn and look to see what he was doing; I caught some of his actions in the rear-view mirror. He seemed to be glancing into the side of our car as he walked by. I didn't need the rear-view mirror to see him now. He was just on the other side of the tinted window. I held my breath and stared straight ahead. I was extremely conscious of my eyeballs in a way I've never been before or since. It took everything in my power not to turn towards him to get a better look, to read the expression on his face. I knew if I moved, he'd see it. I kept my eyes low and used my peripheral vision to see what was going on.

He stopped right at our car and looked in. He didn't get close to the window or put his hands over his eyes to cut any glare, but he definitely gave us a good look over. Could he see us? We didn't know but it didn't matter. We were living our cover and at that moment our cover was that we were not there. The guy moved to the front of the car. He was about six metres in front of us now, and he turned around and stared right at us. We didn't know if he could see us or why he was looking.

My partner and I remained sitting still in total silence. Live your cover. Stay still. Don't move. Don't talk. Don't breathe. He stared for what felt like an eternity; it was probably a couple of seconds. He then turned around and continued walking.

When he was clearly far enough away, my partner turned to me and said, "What the fuck was that?" I had no idea. I said, "You stay right here. I want to see what he could see." I got out of the car and walked around the front to approximately where I thought he'd been standing. There was a faint glare off the windshield from a nearby streetlight; it was still pretty dark and we were dressed in dark clothing. I stared in, looking at my partner, who I knew was sitting in the back seat. I didn't think I could see him. He twitched and I caught it. When he was perfectly still, though, we were okay.

I never did figure out what that guy was after. If I had been in training and someone had pulled that move on me, I would have laughed it off as totally unreasonable. But life happens. People do weird things. It was a good lesson and the car was a nice safe place to learn it. Live your cover, hold your nerve and stay perfectly fucking still.

I realized pretty quickly I wasn't on my regional desk anymore. The work of an intelligence officer doing community interviews and managing human sources is relatively straightforward. At times I'd operated under an alias, but I could be honest about working for CSIS. The people I'd met knew me as Andrew and we would talk openly about my job, what I was working on and what I wanted from them. It had been somewhat natural. As I've mentioned, it was actually with my friends that I did most of my lying.

Special operations was the worst of both worlds. It was the risk of working on behalf of CSIS without the comfort of being able to tell people who we were, what exactly we were looking for or why we were certain places we shouldn't be. If we got caught, we were on our own to come up with a story about who we were and what we were doing. I was raised in the 1980s and loved the movies with fast-talking wise-ass cops or journalists. Think Axel Foley in *Beverly Hills Cop* or Irwin M. "Fletch" Fletcher in the movie *Fletch*. (The name of my university intramural hockey team was Dr. Rosenpenis.) That's actually what I thought being a spy would be like: wigs and moustaches, wallets full of fake IDs. That's not really how living your cover works, though. It's looking like you belong so you never get approached by anyone. If someone sees you at a distance, they should be able to create a story in their mind as to why you are there. If you get approached, you obviously have to explain the story. Ideally it never comes to that.

I quickly graduated from the back of the van to participating in the operations outside of it. This was a combination of the team's growing confidence in me and practicalities. We were a small unit conducting lots of jobs. Everyone needed to pitch in, and we didn't have the benefit of long apprenticeships. Plus, many of these operations were at night, and it was tough to justify the overtime pay for someone who wasn't fully participating. Once I received the course, I was considered fully trained and a full resource that could be deployed.

Most of those tasks outside the vehicle, while important, were not on their own physically demanding or challenging. Stand somewhere and keep watch to make sure nobody sneaks up on the main group carrying out the mission. It was an exercise in attentiveness and patience while blending in to the surroundings so as to not draw attention to yourself or those conducting the operation nearby. I don't smoke, but there were quite a few nights I wished I did. Standing by myself, fiddling away on my phone, trying to look like there was some reason for me to be standing in that spot at that time (typically late at night). A smoke would have been a great excuse. I honestly thought about taking it up. If not a smoke, maybe I was out for a walk or going for a drink, or on my phone trying to connect with a Tinder date. It all depended where I was and what was going on around me. I'd try to blend in, all the while feeling like I had a big "CSIS undercover" sign hanging around my neck. I was comforted by the fact that in all my years of knocking on doors, very few people knew what CSIS was. It would actually be pretty incredible if the first instinct someone had seeing me at night was to think I was a spy.

Sometimes the tasks were more physically involved, and as a rookie I'd get all those assignments. The worst was to serve as a runner. Technology can be temperamental on a job. It's one thing for it to fail; it's quite another when you know it is never going to work in the first place. This happened all the time in big buildings and under-ground garages. The reception was always spotty and, in some cases, non-existent. In those cases, we'd often have someone designated to go up and down stairs to relay information back and forth between the front-line team and perimeter security. It may sound exciting; it wasn't. It was a role we would have given to an intern or summer student if we'd had one of those. Instead, it went to the most junior person on the team. It wasn't a punishment, but it certainly could be punishing.

The challenge of keeping cool and maintaining focus was con-stantly tested outside the van, and none were more challenging than in the case of alarms. I was on another nighttime operation in a quiet suburban Toronto neighbourhood when I experienced this for the first time. It was extremely quiet. The suburbs don't have the same ambient light and noise that a city's downtown has. There is no rum-bling of garbage trucks doing their rounds or young drunk revellers adding background and colour to an evening. In the suburbs at night, everything goes to sleep.

I knew the alarm was coming. Locks assured us he could disable it quickly, but he couldn't stop it from going off. The senior members of the team told me to steady myself for it. They said there was nothing more you could really do to prepare for that first alarm—it was like jumping into ice-cold water. You might know it's going to be cold, but it's still hard to suppress the shriek when it hits you.

As we approached the parked car I was physically braced. My whole body tensed up and my fists were clenched as I saw Locks's hand on the door. I knew it was coming and was still terrified when it triggered. My immediate instinct was to run. It took all the willpower I had to just freeze and wait for it to stop. Ultimately, I knew I couldn't run. Any quick movements would just attract more attention. I was responsible for the security of the team and wouldn't leave them.

It probably took a few seconds for Locks to do his thing. It felt like hours. We all took a deep breath. I looked around. Nothing. No additional lights. No movement. No one looking out of their window. It was amazing. Nobody cared. All my fear of being discovered, and here we were setting off a loud beacon yelling out that something was going on and nobody came running.

The next time a car alarm went off around me on the job it was like I had been swimming in the cold water for a while. I barely flinched. If the neighbours and the owners of the car didn't care, why should I?

Babysitting the Technicians

The next lesson I had to learn was that even adults need some babysitting sometimes. CSIS is like a paramilitary organization with a well-established chain of command along with responsibility and accountability, checks and balances. In human source management I was part of a policy control centre. The special operations security team was similarly the in-the-field quality control for clandestine operations. This included overall responsibility for the security of the mission and the safety of the individuals themselves. Despite them being the most experienced people on the operations, it was my job to look out for the techs, and in many cases look after them.

There was a constant tension between the security team and the techs. In some ways it was like the relationship between James Bond and Q, except in our case Q's devices didn't always work and James Bond's technical ability was closer to that of your average boomer. I am sure the techs were annoyed with us for questioning them when the fact was, we couldn't do what they did. We got annoyed with them if their work didn't meet our expectations, since we were ultimately responsible for the outcome of the job.

I imagine the techs would take offence at my labelling our relationship as babysitting. In fact, I remember when I started thinking how silly it was that this was part of my job and how easy it must be, only to realize how critical and consuming it was. I was like a child thinking my parents were perfect and could do no wrong, only to find out the technicians were fallible characters in their own right. All were great people and competent in their area of expertise, but they did have their odd quirks and personalities that I was expected to manage.

I learned pretty quickly who the guys were with the nervous bladders. Getting in and getting out of an operation was key. We also couldn't leave any trace behind. That meant in-target bathroom use was a no-no. Or at least extremely complicated, involving relieving yourself in a bag and carrying it home with you. Nobody wanted that. Before every mission I would play the role of parent preparing the family for a long road trip. I'd have to work into an operational plan a pre-mission rendezvous spot like a McDonald's parking lot, at which point I could make sure everyone had the chance to go potty.

I would also have to make sure everyone was dressed appropriately. I remember shopping for shoes with my wife around this time. She was trying to find me something stylish, whereas I was checking to make sure they didn't have any tread that would leave marks on a carpet in a target's home. Once again, before every mission I would check my team over in a similar fashion. We needed to look like we belonged where we were going and also that we made sense when travelling as a group. I'm not saying we coordinated outfits, I was just conscious if someone stood out. Any job could involve a computer hacker, who probably didn't own a pair of work boots, and Locks, who almost exclusively wore bright white "dad" running shoes. Think of it like the opposite of the Village People: depending on the job, we could be dressing up like a construction worker, a cowboy or a sailor, but we should all be wearing the same costume.

The techs liked to have fun at our expense too. Their favourite gag for any new IO on the special operations team was to pretend they'd spilled coffee on some important document we were copying. They would pre-soak a fake piece of mail and then pull it out and show it to the new member of the unit, saying there had been a horrible accident. The rest of the techs and special ops veterans would then freak out, selling it like a historic disaster. I admit they got me. It was only a couple weeks into my special ops career and I thought we had screwed up a major national security investigation. I was happy to be on the other side of that gag when the next recruit joined the unit.

For the most part the teams worked well together. However, there were some delicate but crucial conversations when the security team had to assert ourselves as quality control. The techs did the work; the special operations security team had the last word. This was a feature of our separate roles and responsibilities, not a bug. When it came to planting devices and hiding things, if it looked bad—the device wasn't hidden well enough or the area didn't look like it had before we'd got there—we'd have to tell them, "Fix it." This wasn't often, but it did happen. I was sensitive not to stand over someone's shoulder and critique unfinished work. Especially because these guys had been doing their jobs for a lot longer than I'd been doing mine. Inevitably they would shoot back, "I'm not done yet. Don't judge me until it's complete." It was a delicate balance between offending the specialists and making sure it would be acceptable when it came time for final approvals.

If I could tell that they were going in a bad direction and no measure of adjustment would make me happy, I wanted to save everyone time and effort. Time was always tight and starting again sometimes wouldn't be an option if we took too long going down the wrong path. Under the operational constraints we often faced, we didn't have that luxury. There inevitably were some tense standoffs when I thought the work needed to be better and the techs felt it was fine. It can obviously be subjective. It's only wrong when it's been discovered. Ultimately it was the security team's call, and everyone had to fall in line. It probably took just as much nerve to stand up to a tech who had been in the field for twenty years as keeping your cool in the back of a car while someone looks in at you.

The Guy Who Gets You Things

The special operations team wasn't all nighttime missions. In fact, the evening jobs were the final stage of a total operation that involved hours of planning and also procurement of the people, assets and technology required to complete the task. This meant in addition to the thing we were after, there was also typically some recruiting, securing, acquiring or attaining of things that we would need to help us conduct a successful job. I was the guy "who knows how to get things," to steal a line from *The Shawshank Redemption.* Or *The A-Team*'s Faceman.

I did not write this book to give criminals or nefarious foreign state actors any ideas or a leg up on my former colleagues still on the front lines. That is why in the following stories of my time in special operations, some details are intentionally vague or left out altogether. In many ways this is similar to how I had to approach the job itself: even the people I was asking for help were often not provided with the full context for what I needed or why, due to the extreme sensitivity of the operations.

This was the nature of covert procurement, and it was different than community interviews and source meetings. We would be asking people for something we needed to borrow from them—or in some cases access to a location they alone could provide. Locks was pretty good at breaking into places, but if we could convince someone to give us the key, it would save a lot of time and effort.

The items themselves might not be sensitive; it was why we needed them and what we would do with them that made the whole production highly classified. In some ways, this task was easier. Unlike recruiting sources, it did not involve delicate conversations that might incriminate their friend, family member or neighbour. In other ways, covert procurement was extremely challenging. There was often a singularity to what we were asking for: only one location that might work and one person who had the key we needed. The stakes were therefore higher and there was rarely a Plan B.

One of my first covert procurement assignments was to ask a couple to allow me to access their home, alone, for a half a day. I could tell them I was from CSIS, but I couldn't tell them why I needed their home. We also could not allow the couple to be home when we conducted this operation. The target we were interested in, the nature of the threat and the methods and technology we were going to use in their absence to conduct the operation were classified.

I thought back on my first cold call to the home of the suspected member of the Kurdistan Workers' Party and all the scenarios that had played out in my head. I had come a long way since then. I also knew that I still needed a little more guidance.

"What do I tell them?" I asked my supervisor.

"Not too much," he told me. "You can't tell them who you're interested in or what you're going to do in their home."

"What if they ask?" I inquired.

"Be honest. Just tell them you can't tell them."

I thought it was a joke. I thought we would have some elaborate ruse to trick people. We didn't. I was just expected to ask.

I was skeptical about our ability to get the public's assistance without the ability to explain or compel it the way that police and other law enforcement could. I felt like people understood being asked questions about their associates; that was intuitive. Now I was asking for private and extended access to someone's personal residence, when they couldn't be there, and I wouldn't tell them why. I was concerned they wouldn't go for it. However, at this stage of my career I was much more confident in my own abilities. My experience after years in the field had confirmed too many times my underlying belief in the kindness of Canadian citizens for me to think anything was impossible.

Perhaps this is a theme of my CSIS career. At every stage I was constantly amazed at the public's willingness to engage and assist with our efforts. Why would anyone talk to me on background in a community interview? Why would a target of CSIS agree to meet? My requests kept getting more direct, personal and intrusive. Every time I would give my head a shake and think to myself, No way they will go along with this. Then I'd head out the door and learn another lesson on how welcoming, accommodating and supportive people can be.

These were all extremely delicate assignments, and that was the reason why the special operations unit recruited from seasoned investigators. It took all of my experience and resolve built up from years of cold calls to project the self-assuredness I needed to make this request. People pick up on authenticity and they gain comfort from confidence. It's like a stand-up comic who is nervous on stage. They lose the crowd. The audience has to believe in you and feel comfortable with you to relax and go along for the ride. It's no different with a recruitment subject. They have to trust you. To believe you've done this before and there is nothing to be concerned about.

I knocked on the door, introduced myself as Andrew from CSIS and asked if I could have a minute of their time. I knew right away that they were generally receptive to a conversation and had some familiarity with the organization. After some small talk, I got into it. I told them as much of the truth as I could while explaining the sensitive nature of the information I couldn't share. I asked if one day in the near future they would leave me a key to their home, go see an afternoon movie, have dinner and call me before they came back to see if I needed more time. The only thing I had to offer in return for this inconvenience (not to mention the objectively sketchy nature of my request) was to pay for dinner and the movie. I wasn't optimistic.

I explained I was there because of the location of their home. It was deemed to be ideal for the equipment we wanted to use. I assured them they weren't in any trouble and their assistance would be aiding an extremely important national security investigation. I apologized that I couldn't give them any details about the investigation. I briefly went over the mandate of the Service and the types of threats we were concerned about. Their big concern was if they were in any physical danger.

"Why do you need *our* house?" they asked me.

I tried to turn it around from the location to my selection of them and my faith in their willingness to assist.

"Because I believed that *you* would help me," I responded.

"Are we in danger? Is there something wrong in the neighbourhood?"

"Not at all, and I'd like to keep it that way," I responded.

I tried to assuage their apprehension and made sure we spoke about confidentiality and discretion. It was important not to mention safety in the terms of confidentiality. I didn't want to give the impression they would be in danger or trouble if they spoke; rather that it might compromise the effectiveness of our investigation. It was a lot to take in and they asked for some time to consider it.

I'd been in this situation before. The case is strongest when I'm sitting in front of them. It's in our nature to want to help people. It's hard to say no to someone's face; it's much easier over the phone. I was giving them all the reasons why they should help. If left alone they would be free to come up with all the reasons why they shouldn't. I was conscious of the fact I was asking a lot of them and offering very little besides my appreciation and a free night of entertainment. If I came across as pushy, unreasonable or untrustworthy, they could easily have said no. So I focused on the positives: I would really appreciate their assistance, and they would be helping keep Canada safe. I also tried to keep it light: "Hey, you could see an IMAX on the government!"

I didn't want to lay it on too thick. But I did need to press. I didn't have any other options. Although it was true, if I implied this was urgent or that lives depended on their help, they may not have believed me or may have become too afraid to help. "I don't want any trouble" was a constant refrain when looking for assistance. I had to show them that I was willing to work with them. That I had faith in them. I told them to take some time, but not too much. We arranged to meet the next day for a coffee, when I could answer any additional questions they may have and talk logistics. They thanked me for my understanding, and I thanked them for their consideration. I actually left optimistic.

The next day they agreed to help. It was an amazing feeling. In our conversations I had tried my best to remain calm. To pretend that this was all normal for me and I did this every day. I wanted to give them confidence to participate and believe me when I said that I really needed their help. (I did.) That I would do all I could to make it as convenient for them as possible. (I would.) That they weren't in any trouble. (They weren't.) And that this operation would assist a national security investigation. (It absolutely would.) These were all true statements and I sold the shit out of them.

I managed to keep it together until I got to my car. I texted my boss and told him the couple was in. He was happy. I looked around to make sure nobody was looking and gave a self-celebratory fist pump. We intentionally downplayed the importance of these requests to the people we asked. It was only in the quiet moments or as a team that I got to relish the victories. I took a moment and allowed myself to enjoy this one.

Not every case was an instant success. Most people started out reluctant. Some were eventually convinced to assist and others not. Building rapport and trust was extremely important, and in the short operational window we didn't always have the time to build up enough goodwill over coffee. I admit I sometimes had to lay on the guilt pretty thick.

"These are important national security investigations!"

"Do you love Canada?"

"Do you want anything bad to happen here?"

"We're on the same team here. I need your help to stop the bad guys."

"You are the only one who can help us."

I never resorted to threats. I had no enforcement powers or anything to back them up with. Plus, I just don't think I could "sell" threatening. It wouldn't come across as sincere or menacing. It was always a plea for help, the promise of making a difference and the assurance of the nobility of the cause. There were a few times that reluctance hardened to a full no, but more often than not I got the help we needed.

Covert procurement wasn't always requesting help—sometimes it was just getting something and obscuring that the item was to be used by CSIS. I got one request for a storage locker. We needed to keep some equipment off site and wanted power so we could charge and work with it. In this case we were prepared to pay for the locker, but we didn't want the facility to know the contents belonged to CSIS.

I'd never rented a locker before. A few of us called around to see if we could find a unit with the size and power requirements. I thought it was a straightforward question: Is there an outlet in the locker? It didn't occur to me or anyone else on the team that storage rentals would want to know what we were going to be using the power for. (I later learned that some people try to run businesses out of lockers, which is not always allowed and can run up large energy bills.)

When the storage place asked my colleague what we were powering, she was so concerned about concealing who we were and what we were doing that she made up a worse alternative. She blurted out, "A freezer." We all knew what it sounded like the minute she said it. The response was an obvious joke: "What, are you chopping up bodies to keep in there?"

It was not a great answer. Sure enough, when we went in to rent the unit, the person at the front called out to her colleague in the back of the office, "Jimmy, those people going to be keeping chopped bodies in the locker are here." They handed us the keys and we all had a laugh. While our true identities were concealed, it was a little more attention than we were hoping for.

9

WAIT, I'M IN CHARGE?

WITH EACH successful operation I got more comfortable in the unit, and just as importantly my team and management grew more comfortable with me. I graduated from the back of the van to driving the van, from scouting areas during prep to a sentry duty on the mission itself. Eventually I would be with the core team in the main thrust of the job, leading the technicians into the objective area and standing beside them keeping them safe while they did their work. The final ascension was to team lead—the Number One position—and being responsible for the whole thing.

I was nervous for every mission, but especially so when I started on the team. It helped that initially my duties were small and manageable. I also took my cues from the senior members of the unit, in particular the leads on any job. They were such professionals, always in control and focused. It gave me confidence even if I wasn't as sure how things were going.

That was now my job. As the lead I was ultimately accountable for the overall success of the mission and the safety and security of my teammates, who were also my close friends. I felt a lot of pressure to lead by the example I had been given. The team leads I'd learned from and looked up to were always calm and composed. Their skill and poise gave me confidence. I'd benefited so much from the leadership of those before me and felt the responsibility to provide it for everyone who would now be under my care.

The Call for Assistance

It wasn't long into the team lead phase of my special operations career when I got a very last-minute request to conduct an operation against the vehicle of a target. His threat-related activities were ramping up. There was also the added consideration that we believed he would likely soon be on the radar of the RCMP. Once that happened, it would be difficult to get the same kind of access.

CSIS and the RCMP have different mandates and thus separate powers and authorities. Typically, CSIS will become aware of a threat and start their investigation first because of a lower threshold for opening a file. If the RCMP gets on the case, regardless of who got their first, they become the lead agency because they have the enforcement mandate. At that point, CSIS can't just hand the information it collected over to the RCMP. The RCMP has to collect under their own warranted powers and to their own evidentiary standards. For legal reasons, any sharing can be problematic and thus is very controlled.

In circumstances where the RCMP gets involved in an ongoing CSIS investigation, CSIS has to decide whether and how to stay engaged in the file. If they do, this will result in parallel investigations. This may sound redundant, but it's important. At some point the RCMP could decide not to proceed with charges, but the threat may still be up to the threshold CSIS is mandated to investigate.

It is hard to start an investigation back up from scratch, so CSIS tries to stay engaged on the file without getting in the RCMP's way. If it looks like there will be a potential conflict, such as a CSIS source popping up on the RCMP radar, the agencies get together to try to figure out how to deconflict—coordinate operations—without giving away their files and messing up their respective investigations. Needless to say, it can get complicated.

In this case we wanted to move as quickly as possible. It wasn't about getting ahead of the RCMP; we just didn't want to sit around and wait for them or get in their way. Things were happening on the file that were under our mandate, and while the RCMP would take the lead once they got their own paperwork in order, there was no guarantee when that might happen. We simply couldn't risk waiting and losing valuable information as well as our future ability to get this access to an active threat.

I was handed the assignment by my supervisor. I started doing my due diligence on the target and planning the job. In special operations you're further removed from the targets themselves. When I was the field investigator, I knew everything about my guy and even got to meet him. As a service unit to every operational desk, we just didn't have time to follow all the reporting on all active investigations. We operated on a need-to-know basis for our tasks, and we didn't need to know about most of the cases until the request for assistance came through.

I didn't recognize the name of the target and didn't like what I saw. This guy was an Islamist extremist with violent fantasies and didn't seem all that shy about it either. I'd seen a lot of targets in my years at CSIS, and this guy was a particular piece of work. He was a self-professed Al Qaeda and ISIS sympathizer and was interested in conducting attacks in Canada. He was fanatical to the extent that he was angry with other Muslims who were not aligned with his views. He wanted to murder infidels. He hated CSIS. He was paranoid and thought the CIA was after him. He dreamed of bombing a lot of targets in downtown Toronto. He was also a large guy, tall and broad and seemingly capable of inflicting the pain he was fantasizing about.

As was routine, I was also given a picture. It's important to know what the individual looks like to make sure we are targeting—and, depending on the situation, avoiding—the right person. Well, this guy was pretty unsettling to look at. If you were to ask someone what their offensive stereotypical "scary terrorist" might look like, he would fit the description. Black hoodie; long, scraggly beard;

generally dishevelled crop of hair with a slight menacing smirk and knowing flicker in his eye. And this was his driver's licence photo.

I can't say I've been intimidated by many people on the job. I've sat across from some big guys with hateful views over coffee and never thought twice about it. It wasn't just this guy's physical appearance, but also his ideology and the threats he had made (that we knew about). I'm not a mental health professional and I try not to judge people. We have to assess the information we get and manage the threat accordingly, and it's kind of irrelevant to us if someone who carries out an attack based on extremist ideology has an illness. We have to protect against the act—our mandate is not (or was not at the time) to intervene, treat or otherwise proactively address root causes. All this is to say that, from his threats, paranoia and appearance, I did get the sense that there were other issues involved. If anything, that made me feel worse.

According to Plan

The biggest part of leading a mission was actually developing the plan. Regardless of whether the mission would last a few minutes or hours, the planning for the job could take months of prep work. I had a few days.

I knew from the request what they were looking for, so now I had to walk down the hall for a conversation with the techs to find out what they would need and how much time they would take to do the job. This was the critical piece of any plan. A criminal walking into your house and stealing your watch and some cash can take a few minutes. If you want to download the contents of someone's computer—and that person's computer is filled with hours of cat videos—that can take a while. Remarkably, no matter what the operation was, the conversation with the techs always went exactly the same way.

ME: "How much time do you need?"
TECH: "As much time as you can give us."
ME: "But how much time do you need to complete the operation?"
TECH: "We will keep working until you tell us to stop."

This happened every time. I didn't blame them for this response; that didn't mean it wasn't annoying. They were trying to create a large window for themselves, but an unlimited one typically wasn't available. This led to the negotiation and a breakdown and prioritizing of the operation with enough caveats to drive a truck through.

The next ritual conversation was over how much time the techs wanted to prepare.

ME: "When can you be ready?"
TECH: "When is the latest you need us to be ready by?"
ME: (*deep sigh*)
TECH: (*stares straight ahead at me expressionless, honestly waiting for a response*)

Once again, I didn't fault them. They needed time to select and test their gear, then run simulations of the operation to see if it worked. Eventually we would settle on some rough parameters. The reality is that these initial benchmarks could be played with, but they were required so I could formulate a plan and get approvals from our management team. I couldn't just send up an operational plan to the highest levels of CSIS with one sentence outlining our operation stating, "It depends."

The final and probably most consequential conversation didn't involve the techs. It was the "How are we going to actually do this?" conversation. How are we going to get X number of people and X amount of equipment into the house, car, office or condo for X amount of time, and back out again, without being detected? The *what we would need* and *how long it would take* was up to the techs. The *how* was my responsibility. And honestly, that part was the most fun.

As much as I was the lead for the operation, it was very collaborative. I'd pull my Number Two and other members of the team around to brainstorm creative ways to create a time window and exploit it. What looks normal during the day? What looks reasonable at night? What are the habits of the target? It's a riddle or a puzzle with no set right answer. We were balancing probabilities: the likelihood of success with the chances of getting caught. We would come up with elaborate ruses. They were almost like practical jokes, and I love practical jokes. I love planning them and thinking about the other person's reaction. The only difference was the stakes. At the end of a practical joke, you'd let the victim in on the whole thing. Here they could never know we were ever there.

The Keys to the Operation

There was usually a covert procurement angle to every special operation, and a car job was one of the more straightforward. We needed a test vehicle. Think of a pilot learning to fly. Often they will start with an airplane simulator. The pilots run tests on the simulator to deal with situations they may encounter. Techs also needed to practise and troubleshoot. They wanted to test their equipment to see if it would work in a similar setting. That meant they needed something to practise on, and it was my job to procure it. Sometimes that was easy. Sometimes not so much.

I am not a car guy. I don't really care about cars or know much about them—that changed when I joined special operations.

The techs wanted to practise on the exact same make and model vehicle that they would be working on for the job. They didn't want to walk up to a car blind and be surprised by what they might find. They often only had minutes to do their work; usually it was done in the dark, and they were limited to the tools they were carrying to make any adjustments or modifications on the fly. The more familiarity they had, the quicker and better the operation could be.

My job was to get them a similar car. I was constantly on car sites researching makes and models of all types of vehicles, from brand new luxury cars to late 1990s or early 2000s beaters. I was not only looking for the same year as our target vehicle; I had to determine if it was the sport package or there were any aftermarket additions or modifications made to it. I researched electrical upgrades and design modifications, as the impact these changes have on vehicle performance and layout matter. The closer the better because, even within the same year, some car models can change, and I wanted to give the techs the best chance of success. If we opened the door and the car looked drastically different, it could screw up the whole operation. If things didn't work, it was on me.

All covert procurement could be a challenge, especially operating with a limited budget. Unlike the movies, there wasn't some sort of underground Batman bunker that had every gadget, gizmo and tool to use at our disposal. Special operations were already expensive in terms of the resources required to do the job: people hours, overtime, the specialized equipment. If we needed something, we often had to go and get it ourselves with little money and our own ingenuity. It was often very basic and personal. We weren't above asking our co-workers to borrow their car. There was one target vehicle that was the same make and model as my brother's. I casually inquired at one Sunday night family dinner what year his was. It was off by a couple years, so it wasn't going to work.

In the case of the car for this operation, I was fortunate to be in Toronto, which has a large enough geographic area to search in. It also was not as though this or many vehicles we were after were limited edition luxury vehicles where there were one or two in the world. Most were common everyday cars, and the exercise was to narrow down the make, model, year, package, interior and aftermarket changes to get the best fit.

I actually got extremely lucky and found the exact car I needed on a private sale ad on Kijiji. It was pretty beat up and listed for a few hundred bucks. At that price I was worried I'd have to tow it off the lot, which would have been more expensive than the car itself. I called the guy and made my way out to complete the sale. He assured me it would run and could not have been nicer. He then asked me how much I wanted him to write down on the sales slip. He knew that when I registered the vehicle, I'd have to pay tax, and he was happy to write a lower number on the slip to save me a few bucks. Once again this was a cheap car so I assumed he thought I could use the money and would appreciate the gesture. I did; I also knew it would cause a headache with our finance department. Everything needed receipts. We could spend money on some weird stuff, but we'd need some sort of receipt or invoice to get reimbursed. It was like the movie *Munich*, where the Mossad agent is always asking for receipts. It was played that way for humour; nevertheless, it is a very true depiction of the bureaucracy of spy work. It wasn't as though the receipts would be made out to our real names or real organizations;

the amounts just needed to match up. In that moment, I could only think about our finance desk quizzing me on why I said the car cost X but the receipt actually said Y.

This guy was trying to do me a favour; it was actually going to complicate my life. I told him he could put the full amount on the receipt. He said, "You sure?" I told him that I was splitting the cost with some people and I just wanted to have a record of the transaction so nobody would accuse me of getting a deal and pocketing the money. He didn't seem convinced. He gave me a real curious look and said, "What are you, CRA?" I shook my head. "Not exactly."

Surveying the Area

I handed the test vehicle over to the techs. Next I went to check out the area where we were going to be conducting the operation. You don't want to walk into a place for the first time when you do the job. In this case spies aren't unlike common criminals who typically also "case the joint" before a robbery. Ideally, we would survey an area on the exact day of the week we would be conducting the operation. We might try to do multiple days to give ourselves a few options. We were trying to understand the environment we'd be operating in as much as possible. A Tuesday night is much different from a Friday night. If garbage day is Wednesday, then people may be putting their bins out late on Tuesday.

For this operation, though, we were getting tight on time. At this point we effectively had two days. One to plan, and one to carry out the mission. It was an extremely tight window with no backup day.

I went out to the area late that night (which was actually the morning of operation). It was about twenty-five minutes from downtown Toronto. I had never been there before and was pleasantly surprised with what I found. It was typical of the suburbs. The set-up was mirrored up and down the long straight street: a two-storey home with a driveway and small front lawn, and almost all of them had at least one car parked in front of a closed garage.

The vehicle we were interested in was in the target's driveway, which was effectively shared with the home next door. The neighbour's own car was parked beside it, almost evenly away from the house, leaving a great operational laneway between the cars that we could duck into while we did our work. The lights above both garages were off. I tested them and they didn't appear to be motion activated. It was an ideal set-up, although I couldn't be sure that it would be the same configuration the next day.

The neighbourhood itself was quiet and tree-lined, which kept it dark and provided lots of natural cover from the view of nearby houses. There was plenty of street parking too. More importantly, a few cars appeared to have been left out overnight. We would be able to get a spot close to the house and not stand out parked on a totally empty street. It all looked good. The team and management agreed. My plan was approved. Of course, nothing was ever as straightforward as we thought. Ever. In a few hours I'd be sitting in the front seat of the passenger van about to embark on the longest night of my career.

I Was Never Here

The night of the operation was similar to many we'd done before. We gathered at the office around 11:30 p.m. with the aim of hitting the road at midnight. I'd typically try to have a nap before a nighttime job. I needed one that day because I had been up until about 4 a.m. conducting my survey. My wife understood, but when we eventually had a baby, I'm not sure she loved my evening naps and abdication of bedtime parenting assistance.

All of our gear was kept at the office. We had lockers for our clothes and the equipment we might need. The clothes weren't special, just jeans and sweatshirts. I had a T-shirt I wore on every job. I'd found it in a Winners near where I used to live downtown, just as I'd started on the team. It was a grey shirt with white block lettering that said, "I was never here." I'd never seen one like it before and haven't since. It became my lucky T-shirt and a mantra for me. I wore it to every special ops job I ever did. Other items in my locker were things like a hat, latex or heavier gloves, a junky but dependable digital watch with a timer on it, flashlights, allergy medicine, clean shoes with no tread and my go bag to hold things in. In my case, my go bag was a fanny pack. Not the coolest of bags, but it was big enough to hold everything and small enough to hide under a bulky sweatshirt.

I actually learned a lot in the army that translated well as important concepts for special operations. The biggest takeaway: everything should have a designated place where you can find it. Like most army lessons, we were taught this one the hard way. During basic training my most dreaded activity was called a "dress parade." The sergeant major would line up all the new recruits in uniform in front of our immaculate cots and neatly packed away equipment. He would say, "You now have two minutes to get ready for physical fitness"—which meant putting on shorts, T-shirts and running shoes and getting back into formation. We'd all run back to our gear, throw it on and throw our uniforms in piles around our bunks in a best effort to accomplish our task, which we would have no hope of achieving. Now all lined up huffing and puffing, the sergeant major would inform us, "You didn't make it. I want you back in your uniforms wearing your raincoats. Two minutes. *Go!*" We'd run back to our cots, throw our gym stuff around, try to sort out our uniforms (which were now inside out in clumpy piles) and try to find our raincoats buried somewhere in our neatly packed rucksacks. We wouldn't make that time either.

This activity would go on for some time depending on how sadistic the sergeant major was. We'd continue getting in and out of dress, realizing each time how important it was to have things pre-organized for more ready access. The lesson was, know where your shit is. Put stuff back where it should be so you have it ready to go next time you need it. My fanny-pack go bag was no different. Everything in its place, easy to find under stress and in the dark.

We also had general equipment we could use depending on the requirement of the mission. Radios, night vision goggles, thermal imaging goggles (heat detecting)—all the cool gadgets you'd expect. We wouldn't need everything for every job. It depended on what we would be doing and our role in the operation.

We'd get dressed, sort out our equipment and then do a final run-through debrief to confirm the team knew what we were doing on the night. Everyone was expected to have read the plan and know their individual role and responsibilities. It was also important to explain the wider concept of the operations and provide the latest updates on the file and any last-minute changes to the plan. We all had different operations in different stages of development. I might be a One on one job and a Four on someone else's. It might have been a while since the plan was written. It was good practice to refresh everyone's memory and go over it.

The review was low tech and casual. We had those large flip charts in the office, and as the team lead I crudely drew out a rough map of our neighbourhood, what the streets were, where the buildings were in relation to each other, where surveillance would be stationed, how our van would approach, where we would likely park and the location of the target's vehicle. I went over everyone's role and the goals of each person. It was important not to be too prescriptive. I didn't want to tell everyone how to do their job. For example, if someone was on lookout, I wouldn't tell them what tree to stand behind. They could figure that out when they got there. I would simply tell them where I wanted them to look, what they were looking out for and what the expectations were if something happened.

You may have visions from the movies of big screen projectors and annotated street view Google Maps. Not our reality. This was rough and crude and often done very loosely. Some people's drawing skills were better than others. Mine were terrible. I made a note about where the neighbour's vehicle was parked in relation to the target's. In my drawing the cars were as big as the houses. The exercise was to give the team a general lay of the land, not spend a lot of time putting together maps and charts.

The only participants missing from the office brief would be the surveillants. We often used surveillants as additional eyes and ears to help us on the operations. At that point they'd already be deployed to the area. They'd have followed the individual most of the day or at least the evening to make sure we knew what we were walking into. The team lead would be getting updates from the surveillance team and passing them along, such as, "The individual is heading home from work," or, "Looks like the family is going to bed." If there was anything unusual happening, they'd pass that along. The final debrief to the team would include the latest surveillance updates. By that point things were usually quiet and they were just waiting for us to get there.

I remember a legendary surveillance update at one debrief. We were ready to go and search a suspected terrorist's car when we got a report from the surveillance team that the target had gone out in his vehicle. It was unusual so we decided to wait in the office to see what was happening. We sat around a table and listened to the radio updates. The first one came in.

"The subject has picked up a woman off the street."

We assumed it was a prostitute. Surveillance then followed his car to a nearby parking lot where the target and his companion proceeded to have sex in the car. Well, at least he wasn't going over to a girlfriend's house or hotel room, we thought. He would probably still go home afterwards, so we waited ... a while. They were having a good time.

Then, "Looks like they're finishing up."

Great, we thought. The team got up and started to put our gear back on.

"Wait a second, they don't seem to be going home yet ... He's taking her to the McDonald's drive-thru." We sat back down. What a gentleman.

"And now they're parking the car and eating their food."

In addition to the delay and the problems that might cause our operation, we were all sitting around that table thinking about the state of the car that we were planning to break into. It wasn't the nicest or newest model to begin with. The thick smell of fresh sex and stale McDonald's was going to be pretty gross.

On this night, the target was home and the neighbourhood was quiet, so we headed out. Fast-forward a few hours. It was now 1:30 a.m. and I was sitting in the passenger seat of the van. From my humble beginnings at my desk in human source policy, all the way to the front of the van in special operations. I'd gone from correcting policy mistakes to calling the shots. It did feel a little surreal.

The dog walker we'd been waiting on had finally gone home. "All teams, this is One. We're heading out." I turned to the guys sitting in the back of the van. "Let's roll."

The team lead gets out first. We lead from the front. We do the walking, the talking and the decision making. My door was already open when I told the others to start moving, and I was standing by the back door keeping watch as the first crew climbed out of the van. We were live and in the most critical stage of any mission. We were on the move.

It's a lesson learned in training and confirmed in the back of the van: any time you're moving, you're vulnerable. It's when you are moving between areas of cover that you can make noise and attract attention. There's a reason it takes a while to make it out of the van when you first start. That's where bad things can happen and quick decisions get made, so you need to be well trained to handle them.

Although on the move, at this stage we were still not committed. We were just a couple of people getting out of a car. There was nothing linking us to the target or his vehicle. That decision to commit to the operation still had to be made, and that's why the team lead is out front. There is always the option to abort. Just keep on walking.

It would be up to me to make that call. I could see from the van that the target and neighbour vehicles were once again ideally situated beside each other. Now, as we approached the house, I took a moment to look around and confirm everything else was the same as the night before. Were the lights off in the house? Were the neighbours' lights off? Was the street quiet? I had my radio on and I would get updates if anyone was coming up behind me, but I was in the front and only I could see what we were walking into. The techs followed behind. They didn't have radios. They weren't supposed to be listening for trouble or looking around. They were supposed to be thinking about their job and what they needed to do. I would decide. Mine was the only voice and command they needed to hear. Everything else was a distraction.

We walked in a loose casual arrangement, the way you would with your friends. We actually had to practise walking like this in training. There was a weird subconscious default setting that wired us to get in some sort of formation with the leader in front and everyone else trailing behind in almost military precision. If you saw it from afar it would have looked strange. We had to work on our gaggling.

The cover story that night was that we were coming home after a night of drinking. We walked lazily but with purpose, trying to get off the street as fast as possible. We didn't want to look like we were heading directly towards our target; we also didn't want to make a drastic and obvious turn at the last minute. We were getting close to the moment I would be forced to commit—a point where a decision would be made to do the job or keep walking. As we approached the car, I determined everything was as it should have been. It was quiet and we were running late. I turned to the team. "Looks good," I said. We gently veered into the driveway and crouched down beside our target vehicle, taking cover between the driver's side of the target vehicle and the neighbour's car parked in the driveway beside it.

We took a moment to collect ourselves. We were safely out of view at that point, no longer exposed by our movements. We were committed to the driveway, but we hadn't touched anything yet. Now was the time to listen to see if we had made it as quickly and quietly as we hoped. Did a light come on? Did a window open? Was everything still quiet? We sat in total silence. I would be the first and only person to talk. The techs waited quietly for my next instruction. We were good.

I had my Number Two with me beside the car that night. She was a little over five feet tall, smart and one of the most fearless women I've ever met. She was a mentor to me and one of the best special ops security agents I ever worked with. She had been on the approach; her job would be to position herself behind the vehicle, with her back to the street, so she could see the front of the house. She would be the most exposed of all of us. Her role was critical, so it was a risk we had to take. She hunkered down low to make herself as small as possible and hide her silhouette and shadows from any neighbour's view. She got into position and softly over the radio gave me an "All clear."

At that point I nodded to our techs that it was time to begin. I made a soft call out on the radio: "Starting." I looked at my watch and made note of the time. At this point the techs became the stars of the show and it was their time to perform. They had the equipment with them that they needed. They had practised for this exact moment. They silently went to work.

I never knew exactly what they were doing. I wasn't able to help them and I had other responsibilities. My primary job was to look out for them—to keep watch and alert them if there was a problem. I also needed to keep track of their time. I knew how much time they'd told me they'd need. I also knew how much time I thought we had.

This does become a bit of a game: even after all our back and forth during planning, nothing is ever really settled. In the end, I wanted to make sure I had enough room on the back end, so I would typically shorten my time a bit and give them a tighter deadline than we had. They also wanted to make sure they came in under the wire, so they often gave me a bigger window than they truly thought they'd need.

This was supposed to be a short job, so at that moment I wasn't worried about it. We'd done this type of work before and it usually took only a few minutes. Our window was until the sun came up, and that was hours away. Keeping time is much more important for a long job with a lot of moving pieces: making sure there's a list of objectives and keeping everyone on top of achieving each one in the allotted time.

In a job like this, I liked to keep time just because it was so easy to actually lose complete track of it. Any time I was out of the van seconds felt like minutes and minutes felt like hours. Even crouched down with some cover I felt totally exposed. I got antsy and nervous feeling like we'd been there too long. I looked down at my watch to comfort myself. It had only been a couple minutes. My relief was interrupted by a frantic exchange over the radio amongst our surveillance team.

"Someone's coming."

"Is he turning onto our street?"

"Can't tell . . . Yes . . . Yes . . . He's coming your way."

"I got him."

The next thing I heard was the squeal of hard-braking tires and then the thud of a car door.

I peeked my head up from between the cars and could make out what had happened. A car had attempted to turn onto our street. Our surveillant had intercepted him by pulling his car out diagonally into the road, blocking the street and the lane of the oncoming car. It looked like he had only avoided being T-boned by a few metres and a thankfully alert driver (especially given the time of night). To buy us more time, the surveillant had then gotten out of his car to apologize profusely to the oncoming vehicle, claiming that he was having some car trouble.

My van driver had a better view than I did so I asked him how it looked from where he was. He thought the other driver's view was obstructed and we could move without being seen. I gathered the tech team and my Number Two and we retreated back to the van while our visitor was still occupied. As we made our way across the street the surveillant was engaging in what could be called the slowest nine-point turn in recorded history. The driver waited patiently for a while. Finally fed up, he decided to turn, go around the block and come up the other end of the street to his final stop down the block. By that point we were all watching from the comfort of the Dodge Caravan.

We took a few moments as a team to collect ourselves, send thanks over the radio to the whole surveillance team and wait for the neighbourhood to quiet down again. It had been an incredibly brave move by the surveillant. Of course, his own team gave him some good-natured ribbing for risking himself for us lowly special ops guys. We all shook it off as bad luck. As the team lead, I took some comfort in the fact that my perimeter security had held up and nobody had got hurt or caught. The night was still young and we had work to do. After about twenty minutes of quiet, I gave the all clear to head back out again.

We retook our positions around the target vehicle and the techs went back to work. I made another mental note of the time. We still had lots of it. The car was messy but it was manageable. The night was dark and quiet again. Everything was as it should be for another few minutes at least. And that's when I heard Two very quietly saying over the radio, "There's someone at the front door."

I didn't see it. I froze and pushed my earpiece into my ear.

"What?" I asked.

Then again, faintly but very clearly, "There's someone there."

We were maybe six metres away. The only thing between the front door and us was the vehicle. If whoever that was took a few steps out into the driveway, they would have stumbled onto us. And what they would have seen first was Two's head poking out from behind the car to get a better view of the activity at the front door.

I was huddled low between the vehicles, using the target's own car to shield me and the tech team from view. Our responsibility for operational security was to take care of the sensitive equipment and techs first. Should someone approach us, it would therefore have been Two's job to stop or slow them down so I could escort the techs and their gear safely and securely away. It didn't matter if it was a pet, a neighbour or an enraged target. I trusted her implicitly. I desperately hoped it wouldn't come to that, but I had to be ready if it did.

At that moment, we were operating slightly outside the bounds of our drunken cover story. If he had just seen us crouching, we could have plausibly been tending to a sick friend who just happened to be in his yard. But if the target had taken five steps out of the house and peeked around to the other side of the car, he would have seen the rear driver-side door open and a couple of guys rummaging through the back of his vehicle. That would be tougher to explain.

I couldn't see what was going on at the front of the house. I didn't need to look. That was Two's job. I was responsible for the techs who at that point had no idea anything was amiss. There had been no noise to alert them, so they had continued working away. I put my hand on the backs of the two people who were with me. They turned, and without making a sound I mouthed the word "Freeze." I didn't even have to say it. The hand on their backs interrupting their work was an indication something was wrong. The look on my face probably told them how bad it was.

When they turned to me to hear my instructions, I could now see we had a more serious problem than I'd thought. One of my guys was holding something we had removed from the car. I looked at him and I looked at what he was holding. It was a big fucking item. It wasn't like a small screw or a piece of paper. It was something you'd notice wasn't there.

I looked at the piece and I thought about the person in the front hallway. Beside me that night was one of our most experienced technicians. He'd probably done more jobs for CSIS than anyone in its history; hundreds, if not a thousand. I was probably just into double digits. I was still the team lead. He also didn't have a radio, so he didn't know what exactly was going on.

He looked at me extremely calmly and said, "Do you think we should put this back in the car, get out of here and come back later?"

He said it so matter-of-factly and so calmly. I will never forget it. He wasn't trying to show me up or tell me what to do. He was offering his thoughts in a time he could tell I was very open to suggestions.

It sounded simple. It was. That doesn't mean it wouldn't have taken me too long to come to the same conclusion. That was the difference of experience.

I gave the order, "Put that back."

I asked over the radio, "Can we get out of here? Will they see us move?"

Unfortunately Two couldn't see the person in the doorway anymore but the light was still on. She kept watch as the car was restored to its natural state. The techs gave me the thumbs up. I whispered over the radio for Two to come around to our side. There was no point leaving her there by herself. We'd get out of there together. We crouched low and practically duck walked out to the sidewalk, slowly emerging upright like the old apes-evolving-to-man classroom posters. We climbed back into the van and took off. That had been too close. We would need more than a few minutes to let the house and neighbourhood quiet down again. Better to do that somewhere else. Surveillance stayed behind to see if anyone came out of the house to inspect the car. Nobody did. The light went off. It was quiet again.

We found a nearby rendezvous point in a McDonald's parking lot. We all took a bathroom break while we assessed our situation. Nobody had come out of the house, so presumably they didn't know we were there. The job wasn't finished, and it had to get done. We'd let the area cool down a bit. We wanted to give whoever was awake in that house time to go back to sleep. We wanted to let things settle. Then we went back.

We took the same approach and resumed our positions at the car. Only at that point it was so late it was getting early. And early isn't good. People get up early and go to work. Kids get up early and wake up their parents. There are also delivery people who work early in the morning. And unbeknownst to us, that morning's flyer delivery was starting to make its way up the street.

This time the car had slipped past our surveillance, and it took them a minute to tell us over the radio. There was some confusion because it was going so slow. They thought it might be a neighbour and had slowed to park down the street. It was assessed to be coming to a rest far enough away that we could continue what we were doing. But it didn't park. It stopped, and someone got out, made a delivery and then got back into their car to continue their way up the street. Instead of speeding away like anyone would on a quiet street with no police or cars to keep it in check, it kept moving slowly but deliberately in our direction. It stopped again and the driver got out again to make more deliveries. It did this a few times until they finally realized what it was. The guy was dropping off flyers at select houses in the neighbourhood. Now he was coming towards us.

That call came in over the radio, and I think I let out a quiet but audible, "What the fuck?" in utter disbelief at this new issue.

That got the attention of the techs, who turned to look at me, waiting for instructions. Our work area was in a more organized state and the threat was farther away so our anxiety level was much more measured. Nevertheless, we were once again crouched beside our target car wondering if someone was going to stumble upon us and blow the operation.

I poked my head out to get a quick look at the delivery vehicle making its way up the street. At that point it was too late to scamper away for a few reasons. First, if we emerged from our hiding position, he might have seen us illuminated in his headlights. He was shining a big heavy-duty floodlight around looking for house numbers. Movement attracts attention, and he definitely could have seen us move and hit us with his high beam. Regardless of our cover story, it would have seemed pretty weird to all of a sudden see a bunch of people on the street at that hour. We didn't want to risk getting confronted.

The larger issue was that we wouldn't have had enough time to finish the job later. We were so close to being done, and I didn't think it would be possible to come back that night or another day—even if we did have another option, which we didn't. I gave the order to hold tight.

We sat quietly between the cars, and Two, who had been at the end of the driveway behind the car, now snuck around us to position herself near the front. She had some cover behind the car but was now only steps away and in direct view of the front door. She was between a rock and a hard place. It was getting light out and she had little cover either way. The immediate threat was the delivery driver, and the car provided the only cover we had. We still needed eyes on the front door, though. We were desperately hoping our friend wouldn't wake up again and come outside. But if he did, we couldn't let him sneak up on us. It left her very exposed. I didn't feel good about it, but I thought it was the best option.

While I was sitting in total silence, scenarios were now running through my head. As I saw it, we had a couple of options if the delivery car stopped at our house. I could emerge from our position of cover, walk up to the driver, intercept the flyers, and pretend (although not say) I was the homeowner. It would give me away, but it would be easier to explain one person rather than the multiple people who were hiding there.

I had the option to ask one of the surveillants to create another distraction. I trusted them and knew they could and would do it. Once again, I'd be sacrificing their anonymity and putting them in harm's way. The driver was inside their perimeter at this point, though, so it might not be as natural as their previous interception. There was also always a concern that if the distraction turned into a confrontation or anything escalated it would bring too much attention to the whole scene. It was early, and people in the houses were probably starting to wake up. I didn't want to bring them to the windows to see any commotion. Yet again, the best option was to stay totally, perfectly still.

We were in hiding mode and we didn't have to move just yet. The light got closer. It was shining over our heads at the house behind us. The car kept driving. He stopped. We could hear him get out and walk past us to the neighbour's front steps. At that point Two had scurried to join us between the parked cars. It was the only cover left. We all huddled together in total silence. The driver dropped off his flyers and got back in his car. We heard it drive away. That had been close. Way too close.

I turned to the senior tech again. "Are you kidding me?" It was a question directed at him but really said to myself, out of disbelief.

He looked at me with total seriousness and deadpanned, "I've never seen that one before." He was as cool as a cucumber.

"Are we done, man?"

"Yup," he replied.

"Then let's get outta here."

In that moment, knowing we were done, some of the tension started to ease. He smiled and I smiled. It was time to go.

It was almost totally light out at that point. There's a big difference in lighting between 1 a.m. and 4 a.m. In the late hours Two could crouch behind the car and while exposed to the street effectively blend into its silhouette and be safe in the shadows. At 4 a.m. there were no more shadows. Light was hitting us all, and as we shuffled once again back out of the driveway, I could start to see just how vulnerable we had been.

The RCMP's warrant was slightly delayed but they got it and did their own special operation on the car. Apparently, they were in and out of there in minutes with no hassle. Lucky them. As for the target, he was eventually found inadmissible to Canada as a threat to national security by the Canada Border Services Agency. He was ordered deported and removed from the country.

This special operation was touch and go but ultimately a success story. And it happens all the time—although usually in a much smoother fashion. Clandestine teams conduct warranted operations to gather intelligence (or evidence if it's law enforcement) that leads to charges or the removal of a national security threat. No bombs went off. Nobody got hurt. I doubt anyone besides the very close followers of Canadian national security would have even heard of the target at all. It's what we were asked to do time and time again, and I didn't care that nobody knew about it—in fact, that's what made it a success. We got in, did the job and got home. In this case, just a little later than I had anticipated.

10

THE BEST JOB
IN THE WORLD

MY TIME in special operations did not revolve around a single case, plot or large group that monopolized all of the Service resources the way larger files like the Toronto 18 or the Via Rail guys had in the past. Rather, at times different individuals in the region rose and fell on the priority list based on the most recent reporting and opportunities that would arise. There wasn't an investigation that we didn't touch in some small way. We were mercenaries brought in on a file to help fill specific intelligence gaps that human sources were not able to report on. For the next two years I was everywhere—and of course never there.

I loved working in the unit. It was an adrenaline rush and a feeling of accomplishment that I may never experience again. The high-stakes covert recruitments, the nighttime missions. I grew extremely close with the members of my security team. We'd have lunch together almost every day and hang out outside of work. I will always owe a debt of gratitude to them for their support in both doing the work and helping me deal with the surrealness of where we worked and what we were asked to do. Even the techs who would occasionally drive me crazy will always be my brothers and sisters for the times we shared and the things we accomplished together. But like any job, special ops had its ups and downs, and like in any family, there were also tough moments with my teammates and siblings. The bureaucracy, the technology and even the weather would at times take some of the joy and fun out of what was an otherwise amazing job.

It's Frickin' Freezing

If I were to point to a single adversary I faced that caused me the most stress, frustration and pain, I'd have to point my finger at the weather. It just so happened that the Toronto winter in 2015 was one of the coldest of all time. It was a polar vortex unlike anything I had ever experienced. Every day was minus twenty. It just wreaked havoc on our missions, equipment and morale.

Weather was always a big consideration when planning an operation. On a nice warm summer night, you are far more likely to get people up late, hanging outside, or worse, sleeping with their windows open. Conversely, rain really can be your best friend. It's not great to work in if you are going somewhere and don't want to get things wet, but it certainly is useful in keeping people indoors and providing some noise cover for any activity outside. Plus, it has a way of washing away traces showing you were there. The worst of the worst weather is cold and snow. That winter we had plenty of both.

It's very hard to not leave any tracks in snow. One night we were planning an entry into the office of a target. It was an industrial park in the suburbs. We knew it would be quiet in the evening. As we headed to our McDonald's pre-operation bathroom break, it started to lightly snow. It didn't look like there was going to be much or that it would stay on the ground, so we continued on. It didn't stop.

At the complex, a pathway that had been cleared earlier that day was now covered with a light dusting of snow. It was enough to leave footprints. Nobody was supposed to be there, and the sight of many footprints leading in and out of the building from the parking lot would be suspicious. If we thought that the snow would be heavier or continue throughout the night, we wouldn't have been as concerned, but the weather wasn't guaranteed to cooperate. It wasn't snowing enough to cover our tracks and it wasn't warm enough for us to be confident the snow would melt and remove the evidence.

There was an option to wait. There is almost always an option to wait. It's tough, though, because when everyone is mobilized and the overtime clock is running, we all would prefer to find a solution than admit that things couldn't be done. These operations were by their nature risky. We built up trust and credibility with our management by conducting successful operations. In the back of our minds, we were always concerned that by admitting something couldn't be done, we would erode that confidence. The next time we proposed a job in winter, they might hold a missed opportunity against us. It wasn't an antagonistic relationship; it was a delicate one.

We did the job as smoothly as we could and got back to our car to survey the damage. It was clear someone had been there. Would it be less noticeable in four hours? We didn't know, and we couldn't take the risk. We had a shovel in the trunk. I didn't want to shovel the entire area if I could avoid it. It might make too much noise and take some time. I didn't want to be in the neighbourhood any longer than I had to. The snow that had been previously cleared was in a large pile beside the path. I tried to see if I could spread some of it from the pile back evenly over the path and around our vehicle. If anyone had been looking it would have appeared quite bizarre. Why is this guy taking snow that has been shovelled and placing it back on the ground? Regardless of the optics, the bigger problem was it wasn't working so well. The snow on the pile had hardened. The snow on the ground was loose. I was putting chunks on the path rather than a dusting that would blend in. The same went for the parking lot and the area around our car. It clearly looked like a uniquely disturbed area compared to the uniform snow cover in the rest of the lot.

I put the shovel back in the trunk and took out a blanket. I thought we could simply smooth over the area to make it look more uniform. We would quietly wipe away our tracks or at least blend them in so you couldn't see a large number of footprints. Once again, if someone was watching they would be curious why someone was now dragging a blanket across the path and parking lot. It looked weird but it worked. It erased the footprints. Any snow that would fall on top of that would be even and mask our presence further.

We were confident, but a few of us went back in the morning just to double check. If it had looked really bad, we'd have needed to try something else. It didn't end up mattering. Enough snow had fallen that our tracks were well covered over. There was no trace except for the wet blanket we still had in the trunk of the car.

Everyone Back in the Van

That office job was a nice respite from the outdoors, especially given the issues we had with the snow. In the middle of that same winter, during the coldest snap, we got a request for another car job. It would be parked in an above-ground residential parking lot in front of the owner's building and some surrounding high rises. This wasn't a particularly nice part of town, and during our survey of the neighbourhood we had seen some vehicle content theft—kids checking car door handles to see if any were open so they could take what was inside. We had also seen some low-level drug dealing happening in the lot and on neighbouring streets.

We briefed the surveillants in advance. Given the layout of the lot and surrounding buildings, a few of them would need to be outside and on foot to establish a good perimeter. They were all extremely professional, and although I'm sure there was some squabbling between them about who would get the assignments to hang outside in the freezing temperatures for an extended period of time, they never raised an objection with us.

That night was worse than we expected. It was bitterly cold. We all had our bulkiest snow jackets and toques on. It would be tough to use the radios with thick gloves, so we went with thin ones or kept our hands buried in our pockets. I felt for the techs. They would have the real challenge. They had to manipulate their equipment in the cold, and I knew they were very concerned the temperatures would affect the gear. The techs liked to build in excuses in case things didn't work. It wasn't unusual for them to say they would have liked more time to test their gear or they didn't have enough advanced knowledge of the target area so they couldn't predict if it would be compatible. I took most of these complaints as a cover-your-ass exercise; I probably had more faith in them than they had in themselves. This night, however, I shared their concern.

As was normal practice, the surveillants would take up their positions first. They are experts at blending in and getting a sense of the area. I didn't want to leave them out there too long because once the area is secure it may not stay that way. Also, it was really fucking cold, and they would look out of place. Nobody would just be hanging around outside on a night like that.

The bulk of our team was waiting nearby for the all clear. It came and we moved into position. We were in a van and drove into the parking lot. We sat for a moment to get a sense of our immediate area. It was clear, so we started to disembark. As team lead, I was riding shotgun. I got out first to provide watch as the techs left the van. With all the extra layers, it took a few moments for everyone to gather themselves.

I was looking to the rear of the van when I heard the driver come over our radio: "Someone's coming." I turned to look to the front and could make out one of our surveillants walking towards us. He gave me a wave and was fidgeting with his earpiece. It looked like he was having technical problems but wanted to tell us something. I told everyone to freeze. This wasn't a good sign and we'd need to see what the issue was before we could continue. He was coming from a good distance and he was all bundled up. He was walking straight towards us, but nothing was coming in over the radio. Maybe everyone's radios were out?

He'd got to about ten metres away when we realized it wasn't a surveillant. It was a drug dealer. He wasn't threatening or in a particular hurry. We had seen this before on an evening survey. Someone pulled up in the proximity of where we'd pulled up and someone else came out to meet them. We'd assumed that you would call to make an appointment and that this activity wouldn't be happening this late or on a night this cold. We were wrong. This guy was a real professional, still vigilantly looking out for potential customers and willing to brave the freezing temperatures to serve them. We didn't stick around long enough to hear what was on offer.

"Everyone back in the van!" I called out.

We piled back in and left the parking lot before he got close enough to negotiate a deal.

Technology Can Break Your Heart

That winter was particularly hard on our equipment, which only added to the existing stress of planning and executing successful operations. There were things I could control as the security team lead—how we staged the operation, what we did, when we did it— ultimately, though, we relied heavily on technological tools and equipment, and that was something I couldn't control. Dealing with management and the techs could be challenging. Yet nothing was as frustrating as dealing with technology that just never seemed to want to cooperate. We were constantly at its mercy. I cannot get into the types of tools we used or what we did with them. I do however want to explain how soul destroying they could be.

Every operation required a choice of what type of device we might use, and each choice involved a trade-off. A lot of the time it felt like there were no good options. My tech guys showed me a device when I first started on the job. It was a little half-inch box of a thing, and they said, "Here's your implant." That's fantastic, I thought. We could hide that anywhere. Then they showed me a brick of what must have been thirty-four D batteries and said, "And here's your power. That should get you a few months." Their message was clear. If you don't find us a power source, we will use batteries. And here's the thing about batteries: small batteries are great for hiding; big batteries last longer. All batteries die.

A number of things can kill a battery. A lot of use obviously is one; so is the cold weather. And did I mention that 2015 was one of the coldest winters in Toronto history? I still shiver thinking about it. We were constantly working because our batteries were dying all over the place. In one rushed case we used a tracking device for a car thinking it would last for months, and a couple weeks later our techs sheepishly came into my office to say that the device was running low. "You said it'd last for six months," I questioned them. "Yes, but it was cold, and they were driving a lot." I was told since we hadn't had the tracking device before, they could only guess on what the usage would be. Apparently with the bad weather the target was walking less so the device was collecting and transmitting much more information than we'd originally thought. It was a double-whammy battery drain. What could I say?

Other devices or software implants would occasionally seize up too, like all technology does from time to time. Think about any time you've had something happen with a phone, modem or computer that can be solved by simply turning it off and starting it back up again. Sometimes our devices would also freeze and need to be restarted. Maybe there was a power surge and they needed to be rebooted or reset. It could be maddening when we'd taken the time and effort to put a device somewhere we didn't have access to, and then it stopped working. The whole point of close-access operations is to hide the device so the target can't find it. That also makes it pretty difficult to get easy access to power it off and back on. Most of the time it just isn't possible.

Submitting an operational plan required a lot of work and approvals. Management would sign off on our recommendations. It hurt our credibility when stuff didn't work the way we said it would. And it was embarrassing to submit a plan for approvals that said, "Breaking into house to hit reset on the device," or, "Changing the batteries on a device we've already placed there." I've definitely written one or two of those.

A dying battery wasn't the worst technology fix operational plan I had to write. I lost one device a day after we implanted it. We had managed to get our hands on a target's computer. It took months of work, some good luck and a few bucks. It was a big coup and I was psyched. The technical guys were able to load it up with lots of great software that would give us all the access we could have ever wanted.

It was then returned to the target (not directly), and I gave myself a pat on the back for a successful operation.

The very next day I was in the bullpen with the techs and I excitedly asked how it was going.

"We lost it," they told me flatly.

"What? No, the computer was returned." I assumed they thought they'd lost the computer since it was no longer in their office.

"We lost the implant," they clarified.

"What do you mean? We just put it in yesterday." What I was really asking was, Who screwed up? I'd literally handed them a computer and gave them unlimited time to make sure everything worked. It was the best they could hope for. Had they not tested it properly? Had they not installed it properly? They understood my disappointment but were unmoved by my pleas.

"There was an operating system patch and we lost it." Nobody was to blame, they shrugged. "That just happens sometimes."

I wasn't a tech, so there wasn't much I could say. I didn't question them often. That doesn't mean I wasn't suspicious at times that they weren't giving me the whole story. I knew we were on the same team, but they also looked out for each other. There was definitely a code among the techs. I knew something was wrong on a job when I could see them huddling together and whispering. They would inevitably emerge from this formation with the explanation to the mission lead about a problem that was nobody's fault but had to be dealt with nonetheless. The tech team's collusion and message control was a standing joke we'd tease them about. They'd laugh it off, in no way denying that was exactly what was happening.

In a way we were at their mercy. I didn't have the technical knowledge to challenge them on their solutions. I was also much less experienced. If they made a request or suggested doing something that I didn't think would work, they'd always come back with some precedent that predated me and claim, "We do this all the time." It was my job to push back, and it was my nature to do so gently. On one freezing cold winter's day spent changing batteries, I lost it.

We were doing a repair job on some gear we had in a friendly location outside. Once again, the batteries had run out due to the weather and an underestimation of their usage requirement. It was a secure area. We took our usual place beside the techs while they did their work, switching out our teams back and forth to give everyone some time to heat up in a car we kept running nearby. I had dressed for my day. I had fur-lined boots, long underwear, heavy gloves—it was still miserable. The conditions, the reason we were there and the fact that it was taking longer that it should have really started to get to me.

Finally, I was informed that everything was fixed and would definitely now last much longer than before. It was a sweet relief. All that was left to do was test the equipment with the gear at the office to make sure everything was relaying well on their side. The techs would test things when they were working on them in place, and it was good to do another test back at the office if we had the chance. It would ensure things were still working and connecting like we needed them to. That way if they weren't, we still had an opportunity to go back to make any tweaks.

I was standing by the equipment waiting for the word to come over the radio. Nothing came. I was all alone at this point. The techs who were with me had now taken shelter to coordinate the live test from the comfort of the car.

"What's going on, guys?" I asked over the radio.

"One second," came the response from the on-site tech.

I waited a few minutes.

"We all done here, guys?" I asked again. "Do you need to come back out to fix anything?"

"No, no, we're good. Should just be a minute. Waiting on the office."

I continued to wait alone for a final confirmation call that never came. I was getting colder and more irate. If something needed to be fixed, they should have been out there working on it with me.

"What's up, guys? What's HQ saying? We need to get back on this?"

There was a long pause. Finally a tech came back to me over the radio.

"HQ's gone to grab a coffee. We're waiting for him to come back. Should be any minute now. Then we can run the test."

"Are you fucking kidding me?" The tech in the office had been sitting on his ass all day waiting for us to be done to run this test. None of our techs on the job had bothered to tell him we were getting close, to get ready for the two minutes we'd need him? The guy hadn't checked in to see if we were close before taking his afternoon coffee break, either. Meanwhile everyone was trying to keep this from me as I was twisting in the frozen wind waiting for an "all clear" call they knew wasn't coming. I was pissed and I let them know it. That was serious tech huddle cover-your-ass bullshit, and I didn't need to be an engineer to know that was one hundred percent their fault. It was cathartic to be so clearly in the right.

The test was ultimately successful and the device was fixed. I rushed back into the heated car to join the rest of the team. My body and mood started to warm up again. That's when the ribbing started in on me. People weren't used to seeing me worked up and they got a kick out of it. We were a close group that worked together a lot. In the moment frustrations were usually either forgotten or brought up to tease each other over coffees or beers. The techs had their quirks and we intelligence officers had ours too. That could lead to some standoffs. But we were still a team, and ultimately nothing was more unifying than a working device.

A Place to Call Home

We weren't always borrowing other people's homes. Sometimes we needed a place of our own, and the special operations security team was responsible for making it happen. We'd refer to these as safe houses; really, that's a catch-all term for any place where meetings or conversations could happen discreetly, with no connection to CSIS. These were unique circumstances. As you can tell from my career, most meetings happen in coffee shops and hotel rooms, but a safe house could be required in the exceptional case where extra security was needed to debrief a human source, or where a fully private and unassociated venue was required to accommodate a particularly sensitive operation.

My job would be to rent or procure an apartment and make sure it looked lived in so as not to draw attention to it. We wouldn't want a property manager or maintenance person to walk in and find a completely empty space. I would need to furnish and regularly visit the place. The furnishings were generally moved around from safe house to safe house. It was a real mishmash of stuff. A lot of it was donated by previous members of the special operations teams, and I contributed items to the collection too. Rather than take things down to the garbage room in my building when I moved condos, I donated them to the safe houses. It was the same for clothes. I think if anyone actually went through the closet in a safe house, they would be surprised to see the range of clothing sizes and styles. These closet props had been accumulating and moving around buildings probably since the 1990s.

Ideally, when setting up a safe house, it would be like a cover story. You'd try to paint a picture of who lived there and decorate and furnish the place accordingly. Over the years that didn't quite stay consistent, though. There'd be lots of men's items, a few women's and this random bag of baby clothes, with no accompanying baby furniture or accessories. There would be minimal food in the fridge (because we didn't want food going bad) and typically a few cans of beer. It actually painted quite a sad picture—which wasn't necessarily bad since it might ward off questions from any inquiring property managers.

Covert procurement was responsible for all aspects of the space. I'd check the mail, clean and generally keep the place looking lived in. For some places, in the wintertime, I'd make sure to stop by more frequently to run the water and flush toilets to keep the pipes from freezing. It didn't require a lot of maintenance, but there was some. We didn't even use the places. They were for source handlers and their sources. We never got any complaints—except for once.

We were closing down a safe house and moving the contents to another location. It was the day before the last meeting was scheduled to occur with the human source. Ideally, we would do this afterwards, but the timing didn't work out. We moved everything out of the place and left two chairs facing each other in the living room so the source and the investigator wouldn't have to sit on the floor for their last conversation. We thought we were being helpful.

Apparently, the source opened the door and saw the apartment empty with only two chairs and thought they were going to get seriously interrogated, or worse. It looked like something straight out of a gangster movie—there may as well have been newspaper or plastic wrap lining the floor. It took a while for the handler to calm the source down.

One Man's Trash

Special operations wasn't all fun and games, though. It also had a dark and smelly side. The least glamorous aspect was obtaining garbage. That old expression "one man's trash is another man's treasure" cannot be talking about literal trash. If there is anything worse than your own garbage, it's going through someone else's.

For a while it seemed like everyone we were investigating had small children and I was just constantly wading through piles of dirty diapers. It was revolting. I joked with my wife that we should start throwing out all of our paper phone and banking statements in our kid's dirty diapers. My feeling was, if I'm going to get spied on or be a victim of fraud, I want that person to have to earn it!

Garbage collection was also the most regulated and administrative of our special operations. CSIS is still a government organization, and health and safety rules applied. There were full hazmat suits, washing stations and procedures we were expected to follow. In typical government fashion, we would have to watch a video about handling garbage safely before we were allowed to go through the trash. This was a requirement. If I were smarter, I would have gotten out of watching that video so I'd never actually have had to do it.

Handling garbage safely was one thing. We also had to consider storing it. In 2008, CSIS got "scolded" by the Supreme Court of Canada for destroying operational notes. In short, a ruling now meant we had to retain every scrap of paper that supported an operational report. Once again, being government, we received training on how to file notes. We were all trained on the proper file folder to use, how to cite the case file, where to take it, what should be included, how long it should be retained for, et cetera.

The requirement to preserve the official record proved a very special challenge for garbage. How were we expected to handle garbage? Should we put it in the file folder? Should we leave it in a freezer? Should there be a special freezer file folder for all garbage collected? Mercifully we never had to go that far in my time there. We found a few receipts and notes that we were able to file regularly. I always thought it would be some kind of justice, though, if a bad guy did put a critical piece of intelligence in a diaper, we found it, then years later, when they made a request to see all evidence held against them, we were able to produce it, let it thaw out and mail it to them.

Not Moving Fast Enough to Catch IP Ghosts

The cleanest and least dangerous part of covert procurement was serving warrants to telecommunications providers to track down subscriber information for phone and internet users. It could also be the most frustrating. In Canada we have a few major telecom companies, but as I learned there are also many small resellers of phone numbers and website hosting services. Tracking down these smaller providers could be incredibly time consuming, and we were already dealing with information that got stale very quickly.

Some legal background: In 2007 Matthew David Spencer was charged with downloading child pornography using peer-to-peer file-sharing software. The police approached the service provider without a search warrant and asked for the information behind Spencer's IP address. The company voluntarily obliged, and that information led to the police getting a search warrant and ultimately finding his computer, resulting in an arrest. However, the Supreme Court found that the police needed a warrant to even get the information from the provider. This was a victory, I suppose, for privacy advocates, but it was a pain in the ass for us (and, I'm assuming, for law enforcement).

The challenge was the amount of paperwork and the time it took for those requests to make it to my briefcase for delivery. In the case of a suspected malicious IP address, it had to be detected and then, after analysis, determined to be malicious. That determination would be documented and approved at senior levels. A warrant or court order would then need to be drafted and sent to a judge for a ruling. Upon approval by a judge, someone would have to draft a memo or request to get the subscriber information for that user. That request would have to be approved at appropriate levels. Then it would be sent to a regional investigator like me to track it down. The regional investigator would conduct their own due diligence to determine who to approach for the underlying information. Many people use the large providers but, as I mentioned, there are a number of small resellers who buy and resell bandwidth and server space to clients. These resellers often do not have offices, only rented cage space in large co-located data centres.

I did my best. I learned quickly not to bother going to the registered office of the hosting business. Instead I'd track down the ultimate owner of the company at home. I made sure to go in the afternoon; even then, there was a seventy-five percent likelihood they were in their pyjamas. I saw a surprisingly large number of people in their pyjamas over the years.

These smaller players were always willing to help and were often more frustrated than I was about the whole situation. Largely for cost reasons they typically didn't keep the information for more than a few days. Depending on how long it took for the request to be approved and get to me and for me to track down the reseller, that underlying subscriber information might be gone. At the very least it would be pretty dated and therefore not as useful or actionable.

It turned into an odd exchange. I'd knock on the door, explain who I was and what I wanted and then get lectured on how bad it was that it took me so long to get there. Didn't I realize how perishable the information was? Did I not understand how these things worked? In my community interviews I often got to pretend that I was all-knowing; with these service providers I had to convince them that I wasn't completely out to lunch.

I know there is a lot of talk about what subscriber information should be available without a warrant and even rules for preserving that underlying information. All I can tell you as the guy on the ground trying to track these things down is that we need to make this process smoother and more efficient. We are chasing things that are moving much faster than we can keep up with. I am not a lawyer. As a practitioner, it was extremely frustrating trying to carry out this function of my duties. I would get the request for assistance and see the date of the call or click that I was trying to track down and realize right away how little chance there was that I would be able to get the relevant information—and even if I could, that it would be useful by the time I did. There simply has to be a better way.

Who's in Charge: When the Plan Changes

At CSIS, there wasn't much we could do about court rulings and occupational health and safety requirements. Sometimes, however, our internal bureaucracy and personality conflicts could make us our own worst enemy. Before we conducted any operation, the plan for the job would go through a very long approval process. Management had to sign off, and they would only do so with input from all stakeholders as well as support from our headquarters counterparts. These were some of the most complicated and risky operations. Employee safety, the secrecy of the investigation and the CSIS reputation could be compromised if any number of things went wrong on a job. Therefore, there were a lot of people and groups within the organization that needed to be on board and have their concerns mitigated.

That is why the approval process for any operation could be contentious. There's a lot of inside baseball that doesn't make for interesting reading. What is important to note is that even after all the horse-trading and compromises, it was generally acknowledged at all levels that things would happen in the course of the operation that we didn't or couldn't account for. Many real-time decisions would have to be made on the ground. When that happened, protocols and procedures existed for the people conducting the operation to make a change. And for the most part, the teams in the field were trusted to make that call. For the most part.

We had a plan in place for a car job in the Windsor area. It was about a four-hour drive from the office in downtown Toronto. We were going to target the vehicle when it would be parked near the individual's home overnight. It was a classic evening job that everyone was happy with. It would turn into anything but. We were already in Windsor when we got some reports that the target was going to be working late that evening and then heading over to his girlfriend's house. If this had been in Toronto, we would have simply aborted the job for that night. Presumably we would have been able to do it another night when the target and car were at home. At that point, however, we were already in Windsor with a large team. It was a big commitment of resources to be wasting and it might have been tough to justify and coordinate getting everyone back out again. We were already there. This was our window. We were staying overnight anyway. We needed a new plan.

We scoped out the target's workplace to see where the car was parked and where he would be for his shift. Let's just say it was a "food outlet" and he was working the counter. He did not have a direct line of sight to his vehicle, but it wasn't very far away. We thought maybe it would be a minute max. That wasn't a great buffer, especially when the person was working and not asleep at home.

We took a few minutes, as a team, to put a new plan together. We were huddling around our car in a suburban parking lot. We got out some pens, paperclips and other items from our bags to make a map on the ground to orient ourselves and make sure we were all on the same page. It was like kids designing plays in the dirt with sticks and pebbles in the middle of a neighbourhood football game.

We would have a member of our team go into the target's workplace to engage him and keep him occupied. Not only would this keep him there but, worst-case scenario, we would also have some sort of warning if he was on the move. We also put precautions in place to secure the area from witnesses or passersby.

I thought it was a reasonable plan that had a better-than-good chance of success. It was the same car. We had the same technical tools; all that had changed was our perimeter security. As the operational team lead, that was my call. I was comfortable with it. I ran it by my boss; she was not.

My boss was back in Toronto. She was aware of the target plan change as I had been in regular contact with her throughout the day to let her know what was happening. I gave her a call and provided the most recent update. We had a suitable alternative that I felt was secure and, given the circumstances—we were out of town, the clock was running, overtime was accumulating—we were going to go for it. I tried to make it sound as though I was briefing, not asking; then my boss started asking questions and I knew I was in trouble. She wanted to see the photo of the paperclips. She asked me about the lighting. This was a cold call gone bad. We were negotiating, and I was losing.

I'd made this phone call in front of the team expecting a quick word of support. I realized right away this was not going to be a conversation either my boss or I wanted to have in front of them. I tucked my head and phone down low into my chest and turned around to give myself some privacy. The act itself revealed to the team that something was wrong. The conversation I was having was worse. There's a reason they say it's sometimes better to ask for forgiveness rather than permission.

I was blunt: "Do you expect me to type this all up on my phone and email you a new plan from the parking lot? It's 10:30 p.m. Are you going to wake up senior management? We don't have that time." She told me to stand down. She needed to get my new plan approved. She wanted to go through the whole process again. I was stunned.

The policy and standard operating procedures state that the team lead has latitude to make adjustments on the fly. We simply couldn't clear every hurdle we encountered with our superiors. If we'd been in Toronto, she may have even known the area and been more comfortable with the variation. We were in Windsor and she was hundreds of kilometres away.

"Give me the big bullets," she said. "I want to look at it."

It wouldn't surprise my boss to read that she had a well-earned reputation as a micromanager. My own personality tends towards deferential. Like with the polygraph: I'm a pleaser. It was a bad mix. She was also a new supervisor on our team. We didn't have a long history working together at that point. A different boss with more familiarity with me and the team may have trusted us to do the job. A more direct intelligence officer with established credibility with his manager might have just done it without asking. That's not who or where we were.

As for the mission at hand, we were running out of time. We thought the target might work until 11:00 or 11:30 and then head over to his girlfriend's house. We didn't know for sure. We did not have a plan for the girlfriend's house. This was our best and likely only chance.

I was in a very uncomfortable position. I had an entire team of people waiting to do this job. I remember it very clearly. About ten of us were in a parking lot a few blocks away from the target's workplace. There were more waiting in cars nearby. The more experienced special operations officers were pleading with me to make the call. They were adamant it was within my authority and they swore they would all stand behind the plan. We needed to go now, they confidently asserted, and I didn't need permission.

On the other end of the phone was my direct supervisor. She was telling me she was going to call management to advise them of the change in plans. I felt I had two options. I could tell my supervisor I was making the call under the powers given to the operational team lead. I could have stated it in a way that implied it was a done deal and I was just advising. I knew that while just going ahead might have solved a short-term problem, it would cause me a lot of headaches going forward. The unit had lots of jobs in the works, and I wanted to be a part of them. I took door number two and asked for permission. I said, "We have a good plan. We are running out of time. Can I go ahead?" My boss said no.

At that point there wasn't much I could do. It's one thing to assert the authority I had; however, I'd effectively conceded that authority when I'd asked if it was okay. After that, I would be disobeying an order.

I looked over at the team and could see how disappointed they were in me. There is a strong bond, a camaraderie in special ops, forged during previous missions and in the trust we all put into each other when we have a job. We do our best for each other whether we are Number One or Five. Up to that moment it had been another bonding moment for our team. We had an obstacle and we'd worked together to come up with a solution. We were proud of that solution and wanted to get it done. The boss was saying no, and in the movies the renegades say "fuck the authorities" and get the job done anyway. That's not what I did. I sided with management. My team took it as a betrayal. It was a lonely feeling in that parking lot.

I tried to explain that we would hear back shortly. They didn't do a great job of hiding their frustration. Mercifully, I did get a call back quickly, but my boss just had more questions. She had been talking to management, and they had their own questions. We couldn't go on like this.

The dejection I saw on my team's face stiffened my spine. I reminded my boss that I didn't need permission; I was simply briefing up to advise. I said we needed to do the job now. I wasn't threatening—if anything, I wanted to give her confidence in me. Asking permission had put the ball back in her court, and since she was not on site it wasn't necessarily a fair thing to ask, especially of a detail-oriented micromanager. I needed to take back some control.

I think her conversation with her own supervisors had probably been as frustrating as mine and that helped get her back on board. She said, "I'm going to tell management that this is happening, and I'll call you back in two minutes with a go." To her credit, she did.

The team rallied. At the end of the day we did want to do the job, and now we were doing it. We got our game faces back on quickly. I was technically the team lead on this job, and typically the lead would be escorting the techs to the target vehicle. However, there were some experienced members on this job and I had to assign myself a different, less glamorous but crucial role for this operation—I would be holding the door.

There wasn't much room between the target and his vehicle. If he decided for whatever reason to go and check his car, it would only be a few seconds before he was on top of us. All that stood between us was his attention span and a building exit door that for fire code reasons could not be locked. We had planned to send someone inside to engage the target in conversation and keep him occupied; if that didn't work, we would need to delay him from stumbling upon us. We tried to back a car up to wedge the other side of the door but there wasn't enough space, and the longer we were back there driving around and making noise, the more likely he was to hear us, which increased the possibility he would come and see what was going on. So, I volunteered myself to stand on the other side of that door and act as a human barricade to keep him or anyone else inside that building. My job was to keep that door closed with him on the other side until the team could complete the mission or get out of the area securely.

It was a pretty simple plan. The target was roughly my size. I thought there was a better than good chance I could hold him off. Looking back, there may have been some unanswered questions that senior management could have grilled us about, given the chance. Even I hadn't really considered what I would actually do if he managed to break through. What I did know was that it was a role I wasn't comfortable delegating to someone else, and given the makeup of my team that night, I was probably physically the best candidate.

I deployed from the van and took my position at the door. I didn't even look back to see what was happening at the car. I had effectively ceded control and oversight of the job to my Number Two. I couldn't run things from where I was, and the nature of the operation meant that if things did go wrong, Two would be responsible for getting everyone out of there. I had gone from the team lead to a literal doorstop. There are no egos on a job. We all had our roles, and for things to work everyone needed to do their part.

I dug my feet into the ground like a sprinter at the start of a race. At first, I put both of my arms straight in front of me. I quickly realized that if someone did try to bust through, they would probably break both my arms and my face. I turned sideways and leaned my whole body into the door—trying to get as much of my shoulder, forearm and opposite hand pressed firmly against it. I didn't wait to brace myself. The minute I got into position I pushed on that closed door as hard as I could. My shoulder hurt; my hands were white from the pressure. I didn't know if or when he might come, so all my energy went into pushing my whole body against that closed door, assuming he could come at any moment. Mercifully he never did.

I heard over the radio the job was going smoothly. The target was still engaged when they started to pack up. Then I was the last one left outside the van. I was still pushing with everything I had until I got the call from Two that everyone was packed up. I peeled off the door quietly and started walking down the laneway to meet the rest of the team.

I rejoined everyone and got the full rundown. The job had gone off without any issues. The person we'd sent inside had kept the individual occupied, and we'd been able to get access to the vehicle without incident or anyone walking up on us. Everything had gone as smoothly as it could. I called my boss to let her know.

We got back to our hotel rooms that night and debriefed over a beer. This was typical, especially when we were on the road. We were staying overnight anyway, and it was always good to have a little time to wind down. We addressed what had happened. The armchair quarterbacks said their piece, and a little venting all around helped get unity restored.

I got back to the office the next day and my boss and I had our own closed-door meeting to hash out what we needed to do differently next time. It was a tough night and there were lessons learned for both of us. We were able to move past it, but some souring was starting to set in.

I didn't become a spy for the glory because I knew there wouldn't be any. Even my closest friends and family would never know what I did, and public acknowledgement wasn't on offer. I imagine if I tried to explain to my wife that we'd had a successful operation and that my critical role had been to hold a door that nobody came through, she would have given me a slightly bemused, "That's nice." My colleagues were the only ones who were there to witness my contribution and give me feedback on the meaning of it all. The minor spats and disagreements didn't linger interpersonally, but over time they definitely added up. The job was stressful and involved sacrifice. I was happy to do that to fight terrorists, but the constant little battles got to me.

To finish this story on a lighter note—and also give a quick example of how bureaucratic being a special operations operator could be—weeks later the team member who had gone into the restaurant to engage the target came sheepishly into the bullpen to ask for a favour. In order to keep the target occupied he had bought a bunch of food. Unfortunately, I can't be more specific on what that was—I can say it was a lot. And it was a pretty random grab bag of stuff. The accounting team didn't like the fact that we hadn't gotten appropriate prior approvals for the expense. They also questioned why he needed so many things and whether he was trying to get the government to subsidize his late-night snack.

This led to a debate with the finance team about whether this food purchase should be expensed as a travel food stipend and count against his eligible per diem. They asked if he'd shared his bounty and who else should be on the hook for the expense and potential per diem clawback. It was silly. His job had been to keep the target busy, so getting him to make or ring up a bunch of food was a totally reasonable solution. I ended up having to write a memo, which was signed off by my management team, stating that the items ordered were an operational requirement and an eligible expense.

Unsecure and Insecure

If I'm totally honest, I have to admit the big and little battles had an effect on my performance at work. I was doing very cool stuff, but it was still a job, one that came with highs and lows of challenge, fulfillment and doubt. The highs were unbelievable. The lows and the minor annoyances stuck with me just as much, if not more. I was serving my country, but my day-to-day accountability was to my supervisor and most of all my team. My original reason for joining CSIS was to make a difference in the world. It was easy to lose sight of that years later when the realities of the job were more front of mind than the purpose behind why I was there. After a while, my motivation came from the expectations and performance of those around me, and in some cases led to decisions I look back on with regret.

We had just completed a nighttime operation planting a listening device. I was not the team lead. I was, however, the most senior member of our special ops team and was mentoring a junior member of our unit who was getting some of his first lead experience. It was a bit messy as to who was responsible and accountable. It wasn't my name on the plan; I was there to look after things and make sure it all went well. In my mind, it had.

We left the building and gathered back at our rendezvous point to make sure everything was working properly. It was late, and we were all tired but still wired from the adrenaline of the job. There was a rush that came from completing an operation. It was in those moments directly afterwards, still together as a group, that we really got to revel in it all. That night not everyone was feeling so good.

The team lead and I checked in with our lead tech. He was hunched over his computer in the back seat of the car showing the screen to a member of his own team. He gave me the thumbs up that the gear was still working and transmitting. I could see, though, that neither of them was totally happy with what they were seeing. I asked again, "Everything okay?"

"Uh, yeah," he replied, in a not very convincing fashion.

I made a good-natured but half-serious joke about the battery already dying and how I looked forward to going back to fix it tomorrow. He looked at me straight, like he was looking for the words to say, and then said, "Nah, I think we're okay."

That really didn't sit well with me. It didn't sit well with the team lead, either. He also picked up the apprehension in the tech's voice. We looked at each other and realized we were going to need to have a conversation. It was time for a team huddle.

The team lead and I climbed into the front seats, turning our bodies to lean over the middle arm rest to engage the techs directly.

"What's wrong?" I asked. "Is it working?"

"Yes, it's working," the lead tech confirmed. He was adamant it was working. "As I was leaving, I thought I felt it wiggle a bit."

"Wiggle?" I asked.

The team lead got right to the point. "What does that mean?"

"I think it might be a little loose," the tech mumbled.

"What?" I snapped back at him. It came out harsher than it should have been.

"No, look, I'm sure it's fine."

I looked at the team lead and he looked at me. This was not a good spot to be in. Our job as security was to check the gear to make sure it was fine. This meant we looked at it. I would have never thought to touch or move the device to test its structural soundness. The techs would have lost their minds, and they would have blamed me forever if it didn't work. If I had, if someone had, we'd now be able to give the tech a second opinion and the reassurance he seemed desperately to need.

That's what would have happened if that conversation had occurred during the operation. It wouldn't have been a problem. We would have taken a few minutes and fixed it. Now we were in the parking lot sitting in our car.

The surveillants were still in the area, though. They were always the last to leave an operational zone. They were covering us as we got out and also kept some eyes on the area to make sure nothing weird happened after we left. They were exposed and waiting on us to give them the all clear that they could leave. It was late and they wanted to go home. When the call didn't come as soon as usual, they decided to check in.

We were all sitting in quiet contemplation when the surveillance team lead called over the radio. "We all good here, guys? Can we get out of here?"

"Hang tight. Just testing the gear," the team lead shot back.

We looked at the tech, who looked back at us. In my mind it all hinged on the lead tech and his recollection of whether the device had wiggled or not. Although it was an option, he knew we didn't want to go back. He didn't want to go back either. I'm sure he was hoping we would spare him from having to make that decision. Though he was brave to mention it, he wasn't willing to commit. And if he wanted us to make the decision for him, we weren't going to. This was the constant balance between the security team and the techs. They were the experts and often had more experience. We were expected to make the final call on things. We relied on them for the information to make informed decisions. In that moment, that's where we were. If he said it was loose, we'd go back. If he said it was fine, we'd let it go.

It was tense in that car. The excitement of a job well done had turned into a standoff. We were annoyed at the tech's indecision, and

I'm sure he was annoyed at us for being annoyed. The team lead looked at me and I looked at the tech and the tech stared back down at his computer screen to make sure the device was still working. He was probably quietly hoping it would fail, to give them an excuse. It was working fine.

At that point we should have gone back. We had the surveillance team in place, and it would have given everyone peace of mind. As the security team, we should have mandated it. We didn't. We accepted his semi-confident reassurance and decided to call it a night. The joy was sucked out of the occasion. At least we were done. We were all on the same page. It didn't wiggle. Everything was fine. Or so we thought.

I didn't sleep great, and clearly the lead tech had a bad night too. I showed up in the office the next morning and got an earful. He had confided up the chain that the device wasn't secure. He was more certain now than he had been in the car that there was a problem, or at least could be one. This was now a huge issue. The equipment is the most important, most top secret, most sensitive part of operations. And in the eyes of management, we had loose gear that could be discovered at any moment by the target.

We got chewed out by the highest levels of regional management and told we would all be working that night to fix the problem. The same team would be assembled. I was initially pissed, and this time I was on the other side, feeling betrayed by a colleague. In my mind the time to make that decision had been in the car, as a team. We totally would have gone back. We had given him the opportunity to speak his mind and he'd made his decision to let it go. What was even worse was he had told management before us. He could have come back the next morning and advised us of his growing concern. Then we all could have huddled again and come up with a plan together. Instead, I felt ambushed.

We went back that night. We'd had all day to calm down and it wasn't as tense as you might think. Ultimately, I respected that the tech was so concerned he'd felt he had to speak up, and I took responsibility for the fact that we should have just fixed it on the spot and not let it go. There was plenty of blame and shame to go around. We had a job to do and we were all professional. Of course, this job did have a new wrinkle, and when we did get back into the operational zone, we all went and stood around that device when he tested it. I watched him put his hand on the equipment and do his best to give it a little jiggle.

"Well?" I asked.

"It's good!" he said, relieved. "I mean, I knew it was good. Just going to put a little more stuff on here to make sure, though."

"Good idea," I said as I let out a bit of a sigh under my breath.

Friends from Out of Town

Any tough talks and stressful stare downs on the job were far out-weighed by the good times. I truly did like and enjoy the company of everyone I worked with. The tense and contentious moments are better stories, but the majority of my time was spent hanging out in the office, writing plans and joking around. There was also a lot of time out of the office sitting in a van surveying an area or waiting for an operation to start just shooting the shit. There was so much "hurry up and wait" time we filled with ribbing, practical jokes and a high esprit de corps.

I remember one night we were going to do a car job in a driveway and the neighbour's front room TV was on. The whole neighbour-hood was dark except for this flashing blue light coming from next door. We assumed someone was there and from that window they had a direct view of where we planned to be working. We couldn't start the job until they were gone. So we waited. And we kept waiting. It was getting late and it was a weeknight. We started to think maybe the person had fallen asleep on the couch.

A surveillant did a walk-by to get a closer look. We called out questions over the radio to help us try to understand the situation. Was the TV channel changing? Were there commercials? What were they watching? Who was in it? The surveillant was relaying whatever information they could as we were trying to look up the TV schedule on our phones to figure out when this person might finally go to sleep.

The initial questions were serious: What was he watching and how long might be left? But the whole exercise degenerated into farce. Was this movie any good? What else was on that he was missing? What kind of cinephile were we dealing with who was staying up until 2 a.m. on a weeknight to finish this movie? It was this funny little moment, though I'm sure you had to be there to fully appreciate it. My point is that we shared many silly moments like this, in the back of the van killing time, enjoying each other's company, while we waited to go to work.

When we needed to move from a casual to an operational state, we'd flip the switch. But there were also times where we got to work in a controlled environment with almost unlimited time. In those operations we could allow ourselves to relax a bit and continue the joking, while doing the jobs that we all greatly enjoyed.

And nothing was more fun and brought the team together like an out-of-town visitor. It didn't happen often, but every once in a while we'd get some advance warning of a target passing through Toronto who didn't live in the city. We would have all the warranted powers and they were going to be on our turf. Much like in sports, the home team always has the advantage.

Visitors took a lot of the guesswork and surveying out of the operational plans. Often we'd have a hotel reservation well in advance. We'd know when they were coming, where they were staying and when they were leaving. Plus, it wasn't the target's house or another location that would be a challenge to access. Hotels were very open public spaces. It was easy to get in, out and around them in large groups, with lots of equipment in bags, without arousing suspicion.

It might be a good moment to quickly make clear that targets were not exclusively young wannabe jihadists, or any specific demographic. Targets of investigation—whether ideologically motivated violent extremists of all stripes, "non-traditional collectors" such as local researchers passing on sensitive or proprietary information to foreign states, or agents from hostile intelligence services conducting local influence operations in support of their own foreign policy objectives—had very diverse backgrounds and profiles. It was largely due to the nature of the time I worked at CSIS and the desks I was assigned to that my investigations mostly revolved around terrorism.

In all target milieus, there could be entrepreneurs, labourers, students, trades, executives and other professionals of all ages and backgrounds. Toronto is a large city with financial service, technology and research hubs, so we had them all. Plus, with many international conventions and gatherings that attract a large number of participants from out of town, we occasionally got targets from other regions passing through, either in their normal course of business or specifically to conduct their threat-related activities here, such as foreign influence campaigns or recruiting. And no matter whether you are a local businessman conducting economic espionage activities on behalf of a foreign intelligence service or a young high school ISIS supporter with dreams of setting off bombs in downtown Toronto, everyone wants to visit Niagara Falls.

Getting Burned in the Departure Lounge

The airport, like hotels, was also a great place to conduct operations because it was a somewhat controlled environment and easy to blend in. The one complicating factor was the high approval and deconfliction required due to the number of agencies with jurisdiction there. Once all the coordination was done, the people on the ground from the many different departments were excellent to work with.

I'll never forget one time when I grabbed a target's suitcase and was carrying it for a search when the handle broke off. It was an old bag and looked beaten up; regardless, I thought the target would notice his handle missing and it would arouse some suspicion. We were being assisted by an agency, and our liaison could see that I was concerned about the situation. He came up to me and said, "You know how many bags we break around here? Don't even worry about it." It was funny and made me feel a little better—but not enough.

Thankfully our techs came to my rescue. They got out the needle and thread and fixed the handle so nobody would ever know there had been anything wrong. Putting things back to their natural state was their specialty and they were good at it. I was happy for their help.

Getting discovered by the target, a neighbour or even a hotel cleaner was always a risk to an operation; thankfully it never happened to me. Getting caught on a job by a friend was a close second, and it took eight years into my career until I was finally busted. Amazingly it would happen in an airport, which had typically been an operational refuge due to its transient patrons and general chaos.

I was at my sister-in-law's wedding brunch. She had just gotten married and some of the couple's closest friends and family were gathered for a midday celebration. The attendees were some of our closest friends and family too, yet only a handful knew where I worked or what I did. I had been to many events like this before and always managed to bluff my way through. And at that point, besides the just-trying-to-be-polite "How's work?" inquiry, nobody really asked me anymore.

I was lucky that the event was a brunch and not a dinner. I was scheduled to work that evening. It would be an unusual 8 p.m. operation. As was typical, my wife had no idea where I was going or what I would be doing, only that I would be out.

All was going fine until I overheard a family friend mention that she would be heading to the airport that night. She lived in Toronto, so this caught me a little off guard. Toronto Pearson is a huge airport. What are the odds? Really good, as it turns out.

I gently inquired, "Where are you going? What time?" It was the same flight I was interested in.

At that point I considered my options. What was the likelihood I'd be seen that night? I was sure the airport would be busy. I could wear a baseball cap or hooded sweatshirt. Maybe she wouldn't notice me. What if she did? Getting caught at the airport would make for a challenging cover story. It's one thing to wander into the same coffee shop. Being at the airport is not very random. Even if I could think of a good excuse, I'd have to deliver it to my friend, and that would take time, focus and energy away from the operation. Also, if she did see me and we'd just had this conversation about her trip, surely she'd be confused as to why I hadn't mentioned I'd be there too.

It was all a little too risky. It's hard enough to track one person in a crowded space. I didn't want to also have to be looking over my shoulder for my friend to make sure I was avoiding her. It would be an obstacle to a successful mission, and I couldn't let her be a distraction.

I decided to confront the issue head-on and deal with it in advance. I pulled my friend and her husband aside at the brunch. I told them, "Look, I work for CSIS. We can have a longer conversation about this, but I need to tell you because you may run into me tonight at the airport and I need for you not to say hi." My friend is Jewish and immediately told me she had a friend who was in the Mossad, so she totally understood. I responded, "Thank you. And we should probably talk about your Mossad friend at some point."

Of course, the next question my friend asked me was, "Is there anything wrong with my plane?"

"No, no, no," I said. "It's okay. I promise."

Despite my best efforts not to let her presence distract me, it certainly did. I wasn't worried about her sneaking up on me; I was conscious of not getting close. She still wasn't supposed to know what I was doing or who I was with. I had now alerted her to my presence and the fact that something was going on. I was trained in the art of blending in and living my cover; she wasn't. It would be natural for her to look around and be inquisitive. I didn't want her to look strange or attract any attention and I thought that would be more likely if our paths crossed. I tried my best to keep my distance.

Everything worked out. We successfully did what we needed to do. When my friend got back from her trip she said she had seen me at the airport but had kept her distance as instructed. She still teases me a bit for getting caught and not being some invisible super spy. To this day I believe she only saw me because I'd told her I'd be there and she was looking. Nevertheless, it seemed like I'd made the right call.

I did feel bad because I sort of ruined her flight. I couldn't tell her anything about what I was doing, so she assumed the worst. Anytime anyone got up from their seat to go to the bathroom she kind of freaked out a little. I'd said there was nothing to be worried about. Of course, in her mind the fact I was there at all meant there must have been something to worry about. I apologized for causing a stressful flight and said I'd make it up to her over beers—while we talked about that Mossad friend of hers.

11

A DELICATE IMBALANCE

M Y TIME as a field investigator coincided with my single days. I was meeting informants during the day and dating women at night. Basically, I was having non-stop first dates in my professional and personal lives. That all changed when I got married. I started my job in special operations the day I got back from my honeymoon.

My wife and I got married a little later in life and both wanted to have a family. We would have enjoyed having some time together as a married couple but didn't feel like we had that luxury. My special operations career coincided with our attempts to get pregnant. We tried on our own for a while. Months went by and we started getting concerned. Out of everything I ever did in my life and career, trying to have a child was the most stressful and frustrating. There is such a small window each month and then only so many months in the year. One month I had to be away. I felt terrible. She never made me feel bad about it. We were a team on this.

Eventually we sought medical assistance. We got the name of a fertility doctor and started a journey that would include multiple intrauterine inseminations, one round of egg extraction and three rounds of implanting them. Almost every day we'd go for blood tests and ultrasounds. I told my boss what was going on in my life, and she could not have been more supportive. I went to all the appointments. I was last in the office most mornings. I would take days off for procedures. I made it to pretty much everything. This went on for two years.

It was a difficult time, and I didn't realize how many couples struggle with fertility until we went through it and started talking about it. Thankfully our journey had a happy ending. On a break from the treatments with an assist from a fertility acupuncturist, my wife got pregnant. We were ecstatic. And just as I was committed to being there for the treatments, I wasn't going to miss any other important appointments. The first big one was the heartbeat. We were scheduled for an 8:30 a.m. doctor's appointment. The night before, at the last minute, I had to go to Windsor for another overnight operation.

Typically, we would drive down as a group and spend the night. I had other plans. We finished the job at about 3 a.m. I handed all my equipment to a co-worker and asked if they'd take care of it for me. I got in my own car, which I had parked nearby, grabbed a coffee on the road and started to make my way back to Toronto. The regular drive would take four hours. That should have given me plenty of time.

We had just completed a successful operation and I was excited to be getting back. I was pounding coffee and flying down an empty highway. In knowing breach of official CSIS policies and procedures I put my CSIS badge on my lap. If I was going to get pulled over I wanted to get out of that situation as quickly as possible. I was fully prepared to roll down my window and wave my badge at any approaching police officer so they wouldn't even attempt to stop me. It never came to that. The police didn't slow me down—Toronto traffic did.

I hit the city and just got crushed by rush hour traffic making my way downtown. I had hoped I could get home in time to clean myself up a bit for the occasion. I was still wearing my "I was never here" T-shirt—which was beginning to seem prophetic—and the dirty jeans and dark hooded sweatshirt I had used to blend in with my late-night Windsor surroundings. Freshening up was no longer an option.

I thought I might at least be able to pick her up. That wasn't going to work either. I'd have to meet her there.

She called me from the office at 8:25 looking for an update. I was so close. Google Maps said I was eight minutes away. I told my wife to tell the doctors I was running five minutes late and to wait for me. She said no. She was excited, nervous and getting impatient waiting. She said she was going to go in and she'd just let me know what happened.

I had been on the road for almost five hours. I'd walked right out of a special operation into the car. I hadn't slept, showered or brushed my teeth. I felt gross. I was running on adrenaline, coffee and the anticipation of finding out that my child I had waited two years to have was healthy. I had been to every blood and ultrasound appointment. I had done everything I could to be there for this one. I was only five minutes late. It took everything in my power not to throw my phone out the window and scream. I summoned all of the intelligence officer patience and persuasion I had to say as calmly as I could, "I'm really sorry I'm late, but this is important to me. I want to be there with you for this. We're a team here. I'll be there in five minutes. We won't miss our turn. Everything will be okay. Please wait for me."

She said okay. We would laugh about it all later. I was in the room when we heard the heartbeat. It was one of the happiest moments in my life.

Out of Service: When You Can't Phone Home

I hid most of the challenges and aggravations I had at work from my wife. I was working long hours and I couldn't tell her where I was going and what I was doing. Sometimes I'd try to share the little pieces of information I could, but it often didn't make complete sense or lost any substantive meaning with the lack of details. I felt like it would be unfair of me to complain considering all I was keeping from her and asking her to put up with. I'd chosen this career and the special operations desk. I could always go back to the nine-to-five of human source policy or the community interviews of a regional desk. I didn't want to do that either, so I clammed up. I tried to keep things separate as much as I could. The fact that I didn't talk much about work didn't give her much of a chance to talk or vent about it either.

That moment before our heartbeat appointment was an indication that she was keeping her frustrations from me as well. We had been on this fertility journey together, and the night before our big appointment she was alone, worrying about the baby and also the fact that I was doing God knows what in Windsor, then driving alone overnight for hours to get home. I knew I was already asking a lot of her and that she worried about me. Clearly I didn't know just how much.

It was the first time I had seen her really upset with me. And despite my best efforts, I know it boiled over for me at times too. The rhythm and tension of the unit was all consuming. I wouldn't sleep well. There was tremendous buildup to any one job, and even if we were only conducting the actual mission for a few minutes, it could feel like hours. Coming down from the high of a successful operation or stressing out about one that hadn't gone as planned was extremely difficult. I'd get home around four in the morning, do my best to quietly crawl into bed so as not to wake her up and just lie there staring at the ceiling. I'd be physically exhausted, but my heart rate might still be pumping, and my mind was always racing. Had anything happened that I should be worried about? Had everything gone as planned? Did we leave anything behind?

Even the most successful operation could leave doubts. It wouldn't be until we'd hear back from sources or technical intercepts over the next couple of days that we would know if an operation had worked and if we'd managed to do it undetected. In the moment and later that night, we just hoped. This was magnified when I was leading operations—it was all on me. It would be me answering to management on the results. At four in the morning I still didn't know, and that's why I could barely sleep.

There were no sleep-ins either. We had to get back to the office every morning. If anything went wrong or people had questions, I was there in person to answer them. My boss was very understanding with fertility treatments, but for administrative reasons we had to be in the office for regular working hours. This was government, after all. Working late at night qualified us for overtime. It was a perk of the role and we'd rack up the hours. We definitely deserved it; it was nevertheless held against us in a way. We would constantly get snide comments from senior management about how they signed our overtime sheets and saw how much we made. Getting paid overtime meant we needed to also work our regular hours. We were eight-to-four or nine-to-five. And if we were going to claim time and a half for working 10:30 p.m. to 3 a.m., we'd better still be there working our regular hours too.

It could be a grind. I thought I did a decent job keeping my stress and exhaustion from my wife. I didn't want to worry her or blame my job when I was irritable. Sometimes the job did have a way of finding its way home, though. And ironically, when it really manifested itself wasn't when she could see what I was going through, but when she couldn't.

In addition to the radios breaking down on an operation, we could also at times lose all contact with the outside world. Even if we did have working phones, for the most part we'd have to turn them off for the duration of the mission. My wife knew I was unreachable and never gave me a hard time about it. She did like to know when I thought I'd be coming home, just so she had some idea of how long I'd be gone.

Predicting the time for special operations was always a challenge. We had an idea of when we planned to start and how long it should take. There were many nights when we couldn't start "on time" because the neighbourhood wasn't settled yet. Jobs could also run long. Either the gear wasn't working and things were taking longer, or in some cases, things were going great and we wanted to do more and maximize our opportunity.

I tried to give her a best guess. And like a tech, I would pad my timings to leave plenty of room to come in under. I was usually close enough and she didn't notice. Until one time I was very late. And she definitely did.

I was not team lead on this operation. I was given an ancillary role to the main thrust of the job and would be positioned in a building stairwell. It's not a glamorous job. In fact, it's downright boring. Unless something very unexpected or random happened I'd just be hanging out on my own. I thought this would be a quick job. In and out. I took my seat on the stairs and fired up my phone. No service. Shit.

No phone service and dead spots certainly weren't unusual. I was supposed to have it off anyway, so I couldn't complain. The bigger problem was that our operation ran long—much later than I'd thought. It is bad enough to be stuck in a stairwell alone for hours with no entertainment or communication. Worse, I did have company— it was a sinking feeling in my stomach that I was going to be super late, without any way to get a message to my worried wife.

I had told her I'd be home by 3 a.m. I didn't get back to my car until almost 5:30 a.m. As soon as my phone came back to life, it was filled with notifications of missed text messages and voicemails. They were progressively more concerned, and on the last phone call she was in tears. She had woken up at about 4 a.m. and lain in bed unable to reach me, spinning out that the worst things had happened and having no way to get in touch to confirm that I was okay.

I sent her a quick text right away. I didn't want to call in case she had managed to fall back asleep. Of course she hadn't. She called me right away. She was still very upset. I explained that I was fine; I had been stuck in an area that didn't have any phone service. The job had gone long but there were no issues. I was on my way home. I told her to try to get some sleep. I knew she wouldn't be really settled until I got there.

I got back home and apologized for not getting in touch and being late. The truth was I wasn't late, I had just been off on my guess on how long the whole thing would take. In that instant my work and home life collided and wouldn't fully separate again. The strain I put on her became real in a way she had never indicated before. I had been keeping things bottled up from her, and she had been doing the same. I couldn't unsee the hurt and fear that I had caused her. She was now pregnant, and this was an added stress I hadn't really considered. I had selfishly not given it much thought before. I figured she knew I was a spy when she married me, so my lack of communication and unpredictability shouldn't have been a surprise. That was unfair. She hadn't known any more than I had what my life in special operations would be like and how hard that would be on her. Faced with seeing the anxiety and fear she felt that morning, I could no longer pretend it wasn't there, and I knew I was the cause.

No Rest for the Weary

We had our baby while I was still with the special operations team. If I thought working late at night might prepare me for having a kid, I was wrong. Nothing would prepare me for having a kid. Now, my wife did most of the heavy lifting—I wasn't the one getting up every few hours to feed him. I did try to help. I wanted to spend time with him and give her any break I could. The challenge with a newborn is that there is no routine. My sleep schedule was already a mess, and combining the round-the-clock demands of the job and my son meant I was now way past exhausted.

I tried to manage it all. If I knew that I was working at night, I would come home a little early for family time and then excuse myself after dinner for a nap around 8 p.m. I'd wake up, help give my son a bath and put him to sleep. Then around 10:30, as my wife went to sleep, I'd put on my dirty jeans and sweatshirt and head out the door for work. I'd get home at four, try to sleep a couple of hours and then drag myself out of bed to see the baby for a bit in the morning and be at work for nine. I admit there were a few times I'd go to "clean" a safe house during the day and close my eyes for a few minutes.

I was actually lucky during my time in the special operations branch. If we had a couple busy weeks, the senior techs would be sure to regale us juniors with stories of frantic cases and the unimaginable pace of operations in years past when the work never stopped for weeks and months on end. The Toronto 18 case was legendary for the demands and strain it put on the unit. It sounded exhilarating and absolutely punishing.

What also helped was that this period of my special operations career happened to coincide with some of our new members stepping up into leadership roles. I was now able to take a step back and let others I had mentored take on more responsibility. I had enough experience that I knew all the roles and felt comfortable doing them. There could be an hour waiting in a van or at the office before we began the operation. In those moments the team lead was coordinating the troops, assessing the scene and giving us the all clear when it was time to move. I took every opportunity I could to sit down, lean on something and rest my eyes for a minute. If I'd been less experienced, I don't think I would have been calm enough before an operation to allow myself to do that. I was happy to let them run it, and they knew they had someone with experience along with them if things went sideways. It was a nice place to be. It was also probably a sign that the balance had shifted in my life and I was ready for a change.

A Hero to the One Who Matters Most

I never shared the details of my work adventures or misadventures with my wife. She had a general sense if I was frustrated or happy with how an operation went, but I never got the satisfaction of having her see me in action. And nobody leaned over to her at our wedding to say that I had saved their life multiple times.

This changed one day when my son was only a few months old. My wife had taken him to go grocery shopping. He wasn't cooperating, she was frustrated, and in that haze she left her cell phone in the cart at the store. She didn't realize it until later that evening. We called the store and they didn't have it. She was devastated. It had all of our baby pictures on it that we hadn't gotten around to uploading or backing up yet. I fired up my find-my-phone app. The phone was still working. It wasn't in our apartment or the grocery store. It was about forty minutes away, stationary, somewhere in a parking lot near Toronto Pearson International Airport.

It was about 9 p.m. at this point. I could see the phone battery was dying. I didn't have much time. My wife was very conflicted. It was dark and raining steadily. On the one hand, she didn't want me going out alone on some clandestine mission with our baby at home; on the other hand, she desperately wanted her phone back. She was worried anyone who took it might not be so willing to admit it or hand it over. I assured her this was basically what I did for a living: go talk to people and get them to give me something.

I tracked the phone to a trades training facility in Mississauga. It seemed to be in a car parked in a very full, decently lit lot. I had the signal down to about three cars. I tried to peek into each to see if I could see it. I called it to see if it would light up or ring. No luck. I did a quick survey of the lot. Where were the cameras? Where were the entrances and exits of the lot? I was trying to figure out the best place to confront the individual, and where I would move to if something went wrong. I took pictures of the licence plates of the three cars and sent them to a member of my special ops team. This might also be considered a breach of CSIS policy. I didn't ask my teammate to run the plates, I just told him what was going on and that if anything happened, it was probably the owner of one of these cars that had murdered me.

Soon people started to come out. As they got in their cars and drove off, my three suspect cars just happened to be the last ones in the lot. My wife and I were in touch the whole time through the home phone. I explained where I was, and it jogged her memory that there had been some workers in the parking lot of the grocery store. It was my pretext for questioning.

Finally, a driver of one of my cars started to walk towards me. I asked him if he'd been doing any work that day in the grocery store parking lot. He said no and brushed me off. I let him get into his car and moved into my secondary position near the exit of the parking lot. I looked down at my phone to see if there was any movement on the tracer app. As he drove towards me there was none. I moved out of the way. Not the car.

The next to last driver came out. Same question and same answer. Wasn't him. He got in his car, turned it on and sat there for a minute. He asked me what this was about. I told him the scenario: wife at home, baby pictures. He had a car seat in the back of his car. He clearly understood why I was there late at night trying to get the phone back. He also realized that once he left there would only be me and the car with my phone in it left in the lot. He turned his car off and said, "I'm just going to stick around and see how this goes."

I could tell from our conversation he was skeptical that I would get my phone back. I didn't know if he was looking out for me or just curious about how the whole situation would play out. It didn't matter. I now had a Number Two.

The last car was a red pickup truck. The driver came out of the building and headed towards it. I positioned myself between him and his vehicle. I stood non-aggressively waiting for him to come to me, and my Two was sitting quietly in the car beside his.

I was as friendly as I could possibly be. "Hey, were you working down at the grocery store today? My wife lost her phone in a parking lot. I tracked it here to your car. I assumed you found it. Thought I could save you the trouble of trying to track her down. Thanks so much for grabbing it." I laid it all out. No pretext necessary. No introducing CSIS or the mandate. He was either going to help me or he wasn't, and we were going to find out right away.

"Great," he said without hesitation. "I was going to drop it off tomorrow when I went back to work." He rustled around in the back of his truck and handed it over. "I know how annoying it can be to lose a phone."

Phone in hand, I now looked over at my Two, who smiled as he started his car back up. I could tell he was a little disappointed there hadn't been more excitement.

"Thanks, I appreciate it," I told the truck's driver. I shook his hand and walked back to my car. I watched him drive off. I called my wife and texted my teammate in that order.

They both got the exact kind of message I would normally send my supervisor after a successful mission. "Got the phone. No issues. Heading home."

My wife was amazed and incredibly thankful. To her what I had done was brave. I didn't feel that way. I had spent years asking strangers for help. I'd asked them to inform on their friends and family. I'd asked them to give me access to their homes and other personal items without any explanation. Asking for her phone back seemed like a pretty easy job. Regardless, I was certainly happy to be a hero in my wife's eyes. This would be as close to seeing me in action as she would get. I'm glad it was a successful mission.

Winding Down

It was in the quiet moments that my career at CSIS came to an end. There wasn't an incident or one frustrating event that triggered it. It was the daily grind of the job compounded with how increasingly isolating and restrictive it was becoming. The birth of my son made me feel like my world was expanding in amazing ways. Meanwhile, when I looked at my future at CSIS, I felt like my path was narrowing, and I realized that with any move I might make in the organization there were trade-offs I was now less prepared to accept. The fulfillment I was finding in my personal life was in stark contrast to my professional life, where I felt trapped.

The prevailing career trajectory among the senior levels at CSIS was a mirror of our law enforcement cousins. It was a calling. Most of those original classes served for twenty or thirty years and retired from the organization. The founding group of CSIS intelligence officers were Mounties and they were used to going where they were told and moving when they were instructed. Mobility was a fact of life that was to be endured as part of the job.

For others who cared less about the mission of the place, CSIS was simply a great public sector job with interesting work, competitive salaries and a gold-plated pension. Many intelligence officers liked the opportunity to move back to Ottawa, take up a desk job or move into management roles as they raised a family.

If pressed, I would probably fall into the former camp. I'd joined out of a sense of duty. I had no idea what I was getting myself into. It was a swell of patriotism, service, youthful enthusiasm and flexibility. I wanted to serve my country. CSIS offered a unique opportunity to do that, and it didn't matter that I had to be in Ottawa, go learn French or potentially move every couple of years. When I got older and started my family, those things mattered a lot more. I wasn't making independent decisions and I wasn't willing to make the same compromises or sacrifices I once was.

I wasn't afraid they were going to move me against my will to a desolate outpost. Mobility was always looming; the most likely outcome was back to Ottawa. The bigger frustration was that I had no idea when that might be. Any future desk assignment was also unknowable. Even if I could stay in Toronto, staffing decisions were out of my hands. I thought for a while I might like to be the supervisor for the special operations branch. There was only one of those roles and it was taken. I had no guarantees—I could be moved wherever they needed me.

My time at human source policy had had its challenges, and there were lots of desks at CSIS HQ and the region that were less desirable. I'm not against paying my dues and working my way up, but lack of control or predictability in the process or outcomes was starting to feel frustrating. To quote Donald Rumsfeld, there were a lot of "known unknowns" ahead of me in my career, and my previous experience with the human resources department didn't leave me with confidence that I would have support within the organization to help me navigate it all successfully.

The French language requirement was also in the back of my mind. I had barely passed the test when I'd joined, and my skills had significantly eroded since then. My French certification had expired after five years. Nobody was asking me for it again . . . yet. If I wanted to move up, it was something I needed to have. I could put my head down and probably avoid it for a while, but the requirement for French would always be there.

I don't bring this up to sound bitter, only to provide some context. Every job has administrative burdens and annoyances. Yet CSIS has unique challenges that make career planning and advancement harder to navigate. And I wasn't just planning for myself anymore.

Believe it or not, the job also gets old. I was now the CSIS veteran telling the young people that meeting sources in hotel rooms isn't as fun as it once was. Going out at 11 p.m. and sitting in a car until 3 a.m. could be a grind. The fifteen minutes of actual special operations work was still some of the most thrilling and rewarding work I ever did. The long hours of planning, negotiating with techs, managing the bureaucracy and report-writing that went into that fifteen minutes began feeling like more of a burden. I'd get handed an assignment, and rather than focus on the cool stuff I was being asked to do, I was dreading the work that would go into it. I was in one of the best roles in the Service and I was struggling to get excited about it. At that point I probably wasn't going to get excited about much else.

In my mind I was hitting a magic point of no return. I was still in my mid-thirties. I had been with CSIS for about nine years. Where was I going to be at forty? How old was I prepared to be to try a new career? I feared I was becoming increasingly institutionalized at the Service. It was such a specialized job that I worried I wasn't accumulating relevant or applicable skills for other potential careers. I knew the ins and outs of human source policies. I was good at talking to people and recruiting them to be human sources or assist with special operations. I could lead a team to break into houses. It was tough to imagine exactly how those skills were going to help me in the outside world.

I knew I'd be making a big transition wherever I went, and I felt it was better to do that sooner rather than later. Plus, how many years into a CSIS career would I go until it became silly to pass up the benefits and pension? The golden handcuffs are real. We were going to try to have a second child. Who knew how long that would take? Could I move my wife and young family to Ottawa, where we had no family to help? Would it be easier to go when they were older? Or would that be too disruptive? I was getting anxious, and I wanted a little more control over my future.

I started looking back rather than forward. I felt like I'd had a good run. By and large I'd had a blessed career. I'd been given great opportunities and never felt afraid of dealing with my senior managers. I hadn't accomplished everything I wanted at CSIS, but I'd done enough. I was ready to move on.

Breaking Out of the Institution

There is an odd rhythm to a special operation. There is a long lead time to the mission itself, with weeks if not months of prep work. It's a very slow and plodding build to the night of the job. At that point the stress and anxiety ramp up quickly. As you put on the gear, run through the plan and leave the office there is still some joking and teasing, but this is mostly dark humour to ease the growing tension. The moment you leave the van the anxiety gives way to bursts of energy and adrenaline that carry you through the first phase—getting to the target, setting up beside the car, getting into the home or office.

The next phase can include stretches of downtime. If the operation is happening in a house or building, there can actually be long periods when there isn't much happening on the security side. You have the place secure and the tech guys can go to work. The stresses are passed from the security team to the techs. It becomes their show, and you are mostly there to keep them on schedule. For secure operating environments, that could be hours.

The final phase is when the techs are done. There is a tremendous feeling of relief and accomplishment all around. And this is where the real challenge of special operations lies. At that moment of success, when stress gives way and the relief and exhaustion suddenly overtake you, you have to remind yourself that the mission isn't over. You still need to get home.

In this final phase, the security team takes over again, and you need to find a way to ramp that energy and adrenaline back up. It can be extremely difficult. This is when a lot of mistakes can happen. I've accidentally slammed my door hustling into the getaway car, and I've found a stray tool that a tech forgot when packing up their gear in a hurry. It was something we had to constantly remind ourselves: to take just as much care and attention ending a special operation as starting one.

I felt like my CSIS career followed this special operations tempo. There was a tremendously slow build, up to and including my headquarters post in human source policy. The surge of adrenaline and accomplishment was a real high when I was in Toronto region, but the feeling of service and desire to give back faded as I served and gave back. I'd paid my debt or whatever I'd felt I owed or wanted to contribute following 9/11 and 7/7. My belief in the organization didn't waver; my own priorities had changed, and I have to admit I started to crave the freedom to talk about it. Or to at least be more honest.

I didn't want to tell everyone everything that I was doing. I just wanted to have a job where I didn't have to keep so many secrets from people. And to find that job I also felt like I needed to be fully out of CSIS—to tell people where I worked and really give myself a chance to see what was out there. My wife would later tease me about it. She'd say, "It's kinda sad how excited you are to get a LinkedIn account." It was. I was just really excited to reconnect with people, and that started with my family.

My wife was on maternity leave at the time with our son. She was scheduled to go back to work in September. I wanted to have that experience. I decided to quit in June, spend July and August with my new family and start looking for a new job in September. It was a little reckless. I didn't do extensive planning and carefully execute my exit strategy. I felt I needed to pull the bandage off and go for it. Burn the boats, so to speak.

I had a month to tie up loose ends. That meant saying goodbye to work colleagues and professional contacts, some of whom I had grown very close with. Many didn't know my real name, but they knew about my family and had got me a baby gift when my son was born. I would consider them friends. I had to tell them I was leaving, and we would no longer be seeing each other in work or in life. When you're out, you're out. It's awkward and sad.

Looking back, I did everything you weren't supposed to do leaving an operation. I didn't have a plan to leave. I didn't know what I was going to do next. I basically slammed the door and definitely left some tools behind. The difference now was I was no longer worried about being caught. I was done with the sleepless nights. I was out.

12

IN FROM THE COLD

EAVING WAS LIBERATING. I didn't feel like I was turning the page on a chapter in my life, but closing a book and starting another. The adventures of Andrew [REDACTED] were over. The future of Andrew Kirsch was just starting.

CSIS is unique in this way. Most careers don't require such a severe separation. Other jobs allow for general industry and corporate networking that would continue when someone moves from one organization to the next. Not spying. Most sources and contacts I met or worked with in the performance of my duties knew me by my alias. On top of that, maintaining the confidentiality of their relationship with CSIS was paramount. We weren't supposed to know or even acknowledge each other at all in public when we worked together. That didn't change when I left.

My relationship with many of my former colleagues was also affected. I have stayed friends with some of them, but there is a new distance between us. I no longer have security clearance or "need to know" what's happening at the Service. We can't talk openly about what they are working on, and there are new people I don't know who have taken my place on the team. When we get together in groups, I am now on the outside of the inside jokes. It's a world I left and can't fully access again.

Despite everything I left behind, I did gain a lot too. Leaving allowed me to more confidently reconnect with people I hadn't seen in many years. As I've said, I hated lying about what I was doing, so I just avoided most people I couldn't tell the truth to altogether. I had no social media presence. No LinkedIn, Facebook, Twitter, Instagram. Nothing. I was totally off the grid. I didn't want people to know what I was up to, which meant I didn't know what they were up to either. Now that I could be honest, I was excited about getting back in touch. I built back up my professional and most of my personal network from scratch. It was fun, and with my new accounts I missed a lot fewer birthdays.

It was the nature of the job that over the years CSIS pulled me away from many of my friends and acquaintances, both geographically and socially. I naturally gravitated to the people I could be most honest and open with. For almost ten years that was my colleagues, contacts and human sources. That was the other Andrew, and I handed in his identification when I left.

Did I Ever Really Need a Cover Story?

It was strange when I was finally able to be honest about where I worked. The first few times I told someone, I immediately felt a knot of panic in my stomach, like I had just done something wrong. When I was in Ottawa, I sometimes used to say I worked in "aviation security policy." On December 25, 2009, Umar Farouk Abdulmutallab tried to detonate explosives he had hidden in his underwear aboard a flight from Amsterdam to Detroit. (A non-CSIS friend of mine once referred to him as "Fruit of the Boom," a moniker I really think should have caught on.) Anyway, it was very topical, and shortly after this attempt the Canadian government began to explore bringing in enhanced traveller screening to the airports. When people asked me what I did in security, I would tell them, "You know those new body scanners? You're welcome." Then I would explain that I was the guy who had to decide how much shading should be on the private areas. This usually got a laugh from my audience and then I could quickly change the subject. I figured if I was going to lie, I should at least be creative.

The only thing worse than lying to people was telling them the truth and then asking them to lie for you. Putting that burden on someone is asking a lot. And the person I asked to do the most lying was my wife. It just so happened, though, that she was my best cover story. My wife still worked at McDonald's Canada in the marketing department, as she had when we first met. When we were out together inevitably people would ask us what we did. I would quickly chime in, "I work for the government and my wife works at McDonald's."

Well, people's faces just lit up. Everyone has an opinion on McDonald's, and they love to talk about it. Think of all the parties you've been to and all the times you've met someone and had to make small talk. Imagine you could talk about McDonald's. I've heard it all: favourite menu items, questions like why certain items like pizza and the Shamrock Shake aren't available anymore, restaurant-specific memories from childhood and current routines with kids. Even people who hate it love to talk about how much they hate it. I can tell you exactly the number of times I introduced us as working for the government and McDonald's and the person has said, "Tell me more about your government work": zero times.

I almost felt like I owed McDonald's for their cover story. I got a reputation for being a big McCafé coffee booster at the office. As you've probably noticed, if we were planning operations and were looking for a rendezvous point, it would have to be a McDonald's parking lot. I felt like I could show up at home at three in the morning with a hotel receipt in my pocket and not tell my wife where I was and she would be okay. If I had a coffee cup from any other restaurant, however, I'd be cheating.

Having left CSIS and now working full time under my real name, I was free to talk openly at dinner parties about my previous career and give my wife a break from having to carry the conversation. The more open I became, the more I realized how bizarre it was that I'd hid it from everyone for so long. I was sent out to develop trusted relationships with complete strangers over coffee and pulled away from people who I already had those connections with. I had built a network of contacts from scratch and not engaged or leveraged my own.

My intention here is not to throw stones at CSIS. This is a self-criticism—something I feel could have made my own career and life easier to manage. CSIS is not a clandestine organization. In fact, while I was in Ottawa there was a bus stop literally in front of the headquarters office. The bus would turn into the complex and then do a routine stop in front of the main building. Not only was the public coming onto the grounds, but they were actually being forced to. We had a big sign on the gate that said "Canadian Security Intelligence Service." It was impossible to miss.

The advice we were given was not to lie but to practise discretion. I wish I had taken them up on that. I got better, but it was a challenge of working for CSIS that I couldn't reconcile in a way I was comfortable with. I'm sure others have the same struggle. Not everyone is lucky enough to marry someone who works for Mickey D's. "Say you work for the government and change the subject" was not the best cover story. However, in some cases, it may actually have been more vague or evasive than was necessary. I wish I had found a better balance.

Same Doors, New Trick

What do former spies do? I wondered that myself for a while. I told my wife I was done with government and security. I wanted a clean break. I thought of joining or buying a small business. I wanted to be entrepreneurial. I had worked in a bank and then the government. I thought small and nimble could be fun.

My sister-in-law works in talent and development for large organizations. She had a colleague assist me with an executive assessment that is designed to help people find their ideal career by predicting satisfaction and success based on factors such as behavioural traits and competencies. The career coach did not know what I did, so she was as surprised as I was when the test results revealed that my ideal career was doing security for the government.

I ended up working for a new office in the Ontario Public Service called the Office of the Provincial Security Advisor. My wife was supportive but a little confused: "I thought you were done with government and security?" "This is a totally different level of government," I told her semi-jokingly. I did that for a while. My original instincts were right, and it wasn't the best fit.

I then lived a childhood dream of running for office as the Progressive Conservative candidate in the provincial election in 2018 in my home riding of Toronto-St. Paul's. It's where I was born and raised and where I was raising my family. It was also considered a Liberal stronghold. I thought if a big blue wave swept the province, I might be able to ride it to the legislature. The truth is, if anyone thought there was a chance of the PCs winning that seat, they would have had a higher profile candidate than me. It was a long shot; I was honoured to do it and loved every minute of running for office. The seat actually did flip, but it went NDP.

It was a real awakening going from no social media and intentionally keeping a low profile to trying desperately to get the public's attention. I used to lie to people every day about my real name and where I worked, and now there were multiple posters of me with my real name in subway stations. Funnily enough, the core part of campaigning was not dissimilar to my experience at CSIS. There I would knock on a stranger's door and say, "Hello, my name is Andrew. I'm here from CSIS and I need your help." Now I was saying, "Hello, my name is Andrew. I'm here with the PC party and I need your vote." It was so much fun. I'd forgotten how much I missed cold calls and talking with people at their front door.

The one major difference, though, is that when you campaign, they say the aim of door knocking is to identify supporters and non-supporters and get out of there. Don't try to change people's minds. If someone said they weren't going to vote PC, though, the intelligence officer in me was willing to do whatever it took to get to yes. It was a tough habit to break.

I also learned in the course of the campaign—or rather confirmed—that very few people know much about the Canadian Security Intelligence Service. A voter would ask me what I did before politics. When I said worked for CSIS, I would get that familiar blank stare.

Once I told them what that meant, almost everyone was interested to hear that I was a former spy. Most were very curious about what I'd done on the job but assumed I couldn't say. Well, I thought, maybe I could. And . . . maybe I should.

Would You Like to Be a Spy?

The questions I get asked the most are what I did, why I left and whether I recommend applying. I know that you didn't buy this book because you wanted to learn more about me. You're likely interested in Canadian intelligence, want to hear some fun spy stories and maybe are trying to get an answer to that last question for yourself.

I've been conscious not to waste your time with too many non-CSIS-related personal anecdotes. I want to share one more story. If you're considering spying as a career, it may resonate for you.

My wife is a long-time reader of trashy magazines. I admit, since we've been married, I've found them a guilty pleasure too. There is an incredible graphics guy in the Toronto office who is a whiz with Photoshop, which he usually uses for putting together fake logos or working his magic to enhance grainy images to help investigations. He was always incredibly in demand and busy, but since the traditional first-anniversary gift is paper, I asked as a personal favour if he would help me put together a mock magazine cover to superimpose over a real magazine. Rather than the latest celebrity photoshoot and gossip, it would feature pictures of my wife and me with silly headlines about our first year of marriage. He agreed and did an unbelievable job. It looked awesome. And by awesome, I mean hilarious.

I knew if I handed the spoofed magazine to my wife, she would get a kick out of it. I thought the real fun would be if she discovered it on her own. So I swapped out her recent edition, turned it face down and then left it in our hallway for her to discover. It sat there for a few days. Eventually, while I was watching TV in another room, I overheard her in the hallway burst out laughing. It worked perfectly. Please feel free to steal this idea.

I mention this because I think it reveals some of the personality traits that contributed to what I liked about the job, and it may help others decide if they would also enjoy a career in spying. First, this was very low stakes and couldn't really go badly, but there is a certain brazenness (some might call it chutzpah) required to put effort into pranks and elaborate ruses—and, later, into cold calls and operational plans. I enjoy the process of it—thinking up an idea or approach and executing it—even if it doesn't always work as well as I intended. Second, I've always had faith that most people, even busy or more important people, will go out of their way to help if it's for a good cause and they are asked the right way. And third, I firmly believed then, as I do now, that if you try to do things for others, whether for friends or family or in public service, even if you don't directly benefit or get credit, it will come back in some positive way.

I definitely got credit for the gift. But I was comfortable letting my wife discover it on her own even though I missed the gratification of seeing her reaction. It can be tough, though, to put effort into something you are proud of and rely on a private feeling of accomplishment or self-satisfaction. The job definitely tests this at times: not being able to share successes with family, or watching a first date's eyes glaze over as I made my job sound boring. It's a unique challenge of the role, and everyone considering this career will have to evaluate for themselves their ability and willingness to hold their tongue and accept limited public acknowledgement. I realize the irony of saying this in a book. Just know that many, if not most, intelligence officers accomplished far more than I ever did, and nobody will ever hear about it.

"Help Me Close This Book"

When I first thought of writing a memoir, everyone I spoke to in publishing was only interested in my story if it was an exposé of wrongdoing or some sort of salacious tell-all. Well, CSIS is not perfect. Not by a long shot. I mean, I left in part because of some of its many imperfections. But that was not my experience and certainly not the whole story I wanted to tell. Unfortunately, at first it didn't seem like my story was something anyone would want to read.

My next challenge was that even though I wasn't planning on writing a scathing screed, I had concerns I would not be allowed to say anything at all. There hasn't been a CSIS memoir to date for a reason. The CIA has an entire department dedicated to approving manuscripts written by former agents. That type of vetting process doesn't exist in any formal way in Canada. Ever since my swearing in I have been bound by the CSIS Act and the Security of Information Act. I did some research and realized it might be considered a violation to identify *any* person who is or has been engaged in covert information collection. Basically, I might not even be able to tell anyone that *I* had been involved in special operations. That was a problem, since I had already put it on my shiny new LinkedIn profile.

I didn't know what to do: publishers didn't want to publish a book that wasn't scandalous, and CSIS would have grounds to stop a book that was. I was also kind of on my own to deal with it all. It's tough to be a Canadian publisher, and they were quite honest with me—if they got a cease-and-desist letter from the Government of Canada, they were in no financial position to fight it. In that case I would still be liable too. I tried to joke that we could make it a two-book deal and my follow-up would be a memoir from prison. Everyone found that funny, except my wife.

I don't want to get too much into the behind-the-scenes machinations. If you're reading this, clearly I did find a way to get my story out, and please feel free to go online to google whether I'm currently in jail. I bring this up just to note that I didn't set out to write this book because of a promise of fame or financial reward. Neither was really on offer. Ultimately, I decided to sit down and write my story for two reasons.

First, *because* nobody has and, well, I figured someone should. I've talked to a number of ex-colleagues and we all had the same experience. When we decided to apply to CSIS, we tried to find books about what it was like. And there were none. We were reading old RCMP books from the eighties or memoirs of Canadians who'd joined other countries' intelligence services. I wish there had been something like this for me. And of course, now that I'm officially a very public Canadian ex-spy, I get a lot of questions about what it was like, from friends and friends of friends alike. I don't mind having those conversations at all, but now I can just tell them, "Have I got a book for you!"

The second reason is something I've also mentioned before: we can be extremely complacent here in Canada. I was listening to a discussion about national security once, and I heard someone say dismissively that you were more likely to die from getting hit by lightning than from a terrorist attack. I've actually read this fun statistic and heard it regurgitated a few times. It may even be true. But here's the thing: in Canada alone, between CSIS; RCMP; CBSA; Immigration, Refugees and Citizenship; the Communication Security Establishment; the Canadian military; and local law enforcement, thousands and thousands of people are part of a vast, coordinated intelligence-sharing apparatus to make sure that you don't die from a terrorist attack. I don't mean to fear-monger here. What I want to say to everyone who shares that sentiment is to please consider that these statistics aren't evidence that security isn't necessary; rather, they provide evidence that it works.

That is the story I wanted to tell. To share my experience as a part of this community you don't get to hear much about. To explain what I did in my nine years at the Service, what CSIS does more broadly and, just as importantly, what we need from the public to help us do our job. I want to add to the wider conversation about national security and to try to convey that, unfortunately, there are bad people in the world, and one reason Canada remains a safe place to live is because there are people working hard behind their computers, meeting in coffee shops and hotel rooms, and even keeping watch late at night in stairwells and in the shadows so it stays that way.

My wife and I were blessed to have a second child, another boy born two years after our first. I am sad that my two young sons will not get to go to grade nine career day at CSIS, to learn how to pick locks and see where their dad worked. Instead, they can read this book and know that their dad saw some bad stuff going on in the world and wanted to do his part. Some of it was administrative, lonely, frustrating, challenging, intense, rewarding and fun. I signed up because I wanted my kids to grow up in a safer world. I left so that I could enjoying being in that safer world a little more with them.

EPILOGUE

I HOPE I HAVE done a reasonable job of explaining the challenges we faced during my time at CSIS. While violent extremism remains a significant security threat, I'd now like to take a moment to look forward and talk about cyber security, explain why it's a unique challenge and make a final plea for everyone to stay vigilant and do their part to keep each other safe.

It's a big part of what I do now in the risk advisory practice I started when I left the Ontario Public Service. We conduct physical security threat risk assessments and recommend protective controls where we find gaps that can be exploited. I joke that I used to break into places, so I know how to help organizations defend themselves. We also do online exposure risk assessments to determine if an individual's digital footprint and internet activities are creating vulnerabilities in their physical lives. The origins of this cyber security risk relate back to trends that started when I was still doing covert operations.

Breaking Into Phones, Not Homes

The stories that the older techs and special operations IOs told about how much tougher the job was in their day were largely true. They operated in a different era. The close-access team used to have to get near the targets to physically place any listening or tracking equipment in proximity to where we wanted to collect information. Now, everyone carries a microphone, camera and location tracker on them at all times in the form of their phone. All we have to do is get access to the devices to gather the information they are collecting for us.

The transition from close to remote access accelerated throughout my time in the special operations unit. The remote techs were increasingly able to get their hands on the same information as the close-access teams, from behind their computers. It changed the financial cost and risk profile of the operations completely. No more overtime for large teams. Even if we got caught hacking a phone, there was much more plausible deniability than being discovered in someone's house physically holding it.

The unfortunate truth is that for all the reasons that remote access has become a more attractive option for CSIS (and remember, these are the good people), the criminals and malicious foreign states took notice too. I actually witnessed this first-hand. We were sitting in the special operations bullpen one day trying to figure out how to get access to the computer of a target who we were told was very paranoid and technologically sophisticated. We were gaming out expensive and labour-intensive scenarios to break into his home when we were alerted urgently by one of our communications analysts who was listening to his calls. Apparently, the target had just been speaking to someone claiming to be Microsoft tech support, and for the fee of five hundred dollars they would "fix" an issue with his computer. The target agreed. It was amazing. We were listening over the phone as not only did the scammer break into the computer, but also the target actually paid him to do it.

This is the rapidly growing cyber threat we all face today. Online, bad guys aren't restricted to attacking people in their geographic location. They now have access to billions of people all over the world from the comfort of their own keyboard. The cost-benefit analysis of a cyberattack is also much different from that of a common criminal. The amount of time it takes to send a phishing email, and the likelihood of getting caught versus the potential award of having someone click the link, has made hacking an extremely attractive, lucrative and comfortable occupation.

Online Chum to the Cyber Sharks

So how do they get you? Well, in the early days phishing scams were almost quaint in their simplicity. I remember one attack another intelligence service used that included four text messages. They were, in order: naked picture, naked picture, malicious link, "oops that wasn't for you." There was a one hundred percent success rate. Sounds easy, right? Their joke was, "Do you know how many hours were spent selecting those naked pictures to make sure they were the right ones?!"

While we have definitely collectively raised our game from the naked picture texts, Britney Spears computer viruses and Nigerian prince email scams, I'm sorry to report that as our own digital security awareness improves, so does the sophistication of our attackers. We are now up against advanced social-engineering techniques to get us to click links and give up our credentials and sensitive information.

The attackers are aided by another trend that started while I was at CSIS: the explosion of data that is now publicly available about any individual. This can be the information we voluntarily place online about ourselves, but also data that is being collected about us from the apps we use or the internet-connected devices and other technology tools we have in our homes.

Think about all the social media and networking sites that are out there. Facebook launched after I graduated from university and it's already considered the site for boomers. I met my wife online (twice) and even that was before the current crop of sites like Tinder and Bumble. There are probably new ones that have come up in the time I've spent writing this epilogue. I'm not trying to make myself sound old but to highlight these numerous and growing large repositories of information that we continue to populate with details about our business interests, social network, family life and hobbies.

The sheer volume of this personal data available online has also had a dramatic effect on the spy game. It has become essential for recruiting human sources and covert procurement assistance. Back at CSIS, I'd never rely exclusively on my skills on the phone or at the door. In the early days, I would crudely try to profile people from their profession, civic engagement or maybe old newspaper clippings, if I could find any. Now we can see who they are following on Instagram, what they like or retweet and who they are friends with on Facebook or connected to through LinkedIn. All of this helps paint a much better picture when trying to decide who to approach and how. This information is also available to those who wish to do harm. They can find vulnerable individuals with the access they want and then use publicly available information to target and exploit them.

As a quick side note to any future spies out there, this trend will affect how we monitor and assess our subjects of investigation. In addition to human source reporting and technical sources, we will have access to more and more of the target's publicly available information. The challenge will change from trying to get access to it to making sure that we are processing that raw information into good intelligence through sound analysis when assessing a target's threat-related activities.

Spying will always include recruiting and targeting individuals. Both of these pursuits will be increasingly aided and tested by the ever-expanding pervasiveness of the internet in our lives. The next generation of spies will need to have the ability to understand and use technical tools to process, synthesize, analyze and interpret this information for its relevance. My advice to the intelligence officers of the future is to get comfortable navigating this digital space.

Now back to my original point. My advice and plea to everyone else is this: Be careful out there. Because once again, the bad guys are getting better at all of this too.

Stay Vigilant—For Yourself and for All of Us!

At this point, you may be wondering why a former spy is worried about you being phished or scammed online. You also may be thinking you don't have anything of value for anyone to take. And some of you may even think, If they get me, they get me, so why should anyone else care? Well, for one, I don't want to see anyone get cyberstalked or lose money, their identity or worse. Additionally, you absolutely do have valuable information, and more importantly you provide access to your friends, business and wider network online. For some, this could mean access to government secrets and sensitive information. I am writing this in my spy book because even if you aren't interested in taking steps to protect yourself, please do it for your friends, your co-workers and your country.

Don't just take it from me. This is something CSIS has been waving their arms about for the past few years. In the spirit of helping CSIS spread their message (you're welcome!), let me highlight the sentiments expressed in both the CSIS public reports and a 2021 speech given by the current CSIS director: economic espionage activities in Canada by hostile foreign states are having a devastating impact on our prosperity and sovereignty. Our adversaries are intent on stealing our intellectual property and advanced research, whether it be from the Canadian government, large corporations, small start-ups or universities. They are doing this the old-fashioned way by recruiting, coercing and partnering with local witting or unwitting accomplices to gather intelligence that would provide an economic, military or political advantage. They are also increasingly using cyber methods to target and exploit Canada and Canadians.

The ultimate public example of the devastation a state-sponsored remote attack can have on Canadian industry is Nortel, whose market capitalization fell from $398 billion in 2000 to less than $5 billion in 2002. The fall of Nortel has largely been attributed to a large-scale systematic hacking of the company by the Chinese military that was facilitated by them stealing some executive passwords. Reporting in 2020 from Global News and others suggests that Nortel was aware of the risks but dismissed them as "exaggerated spy novel plots." The cold reality is that by taking advantage of a few key individuals with the right access, the hackers were effectively able to destroy a one-time Canadian telecom industry giant.

Organizations need robust physical security controls to protect their people, assets and information. There is a collective need for increased cyber security awareness and vigilance as well. The Nortel case study demonstrates what makes this challenge so difficult to defend. The breaches of large organizations or small start-ups with cutting-edge technology often originate with an individual who has allowed their personal access credentials to be compromised. People can be their company's or government's greatest asset, but they are also its biggest vulnerability. I can recommend high-security locks on a front door. We all have usernames, passwords and logins that can serve as their own keys to our wider and extremely valuable IT networks. Every single day the bad guys are trying to steal all of our keys.

I may no longer work for CSIS, but I still have a role to play in keeping Canada safe and prosperous. We all do—because we are only as strong as our weakest link. We all need to do our part. Bad things may unfortunately still happen. Like millions of people, I was a victim in the Yahoo! hacks. (To the hackers: If you wanted to know my fantasy football roster, you could have just asked.) The key is not to get discouraged. It's an ongoing battle. And while the threats may change, whatever we face, we are stronger and safer when we work together.

I know Canadians are always willing to help if asked. So consider this my knock on your door.

ACKNOWLEDGEMENTS

A FEW APPROPRIATELY security-cleared individuals gave the manuscript or portions of it an early read and subsequent advice. Thank you to [REDACTED], [REDACTED] and [REDACTED]. Any errors of omission or inclusion are mine and mine alone.

To my editors Pam Robertson and Jenny Govier, my designers Taysia Louie and Fiona Lee, and Adrineh Der-Boghossian, Trena White and everyone at Page Two, thank you for all of your assistance. You were a pleasure to work with.

Thank you to my former CSIS colleagues, as well as those who came before me and after. For a short time I was a small part of a large organization made up of extraordinary individuals. I appreciate all that you have done and continue to do. I know how hard the job is and how much you sacrifice to do it. I hope this book captures your dedication and honours your service.

I also owe profound gratitude to those who took my calls, shared a coffee and opened their homes to me. Thank you for your time, advice and assistance. You play the most critical role in keeping Canada safe. You are true heroes who never get the full recognition you deserve.

Thank you to my father who had a love for life and lived the spirit of *carpe diem* he championed for his kids. He encouraged me to follow my own path. He was the best dad anyone could hope for and is the role model for the man and father I hope to be.

My mother instilled in me our family values with her four words—helpful, harmonious, grateful and responsible—and inspired me to a life of service with her professional dedication to the not-for-profit community. Thank you for always supporting me with love and encouragement and always believing that I would find my way.

To my brothers, Greg, J and Matt, and my sisters-in-law Laura, Alison and Natasha, thank you for putting up with me. I look up to you all more than you know. I was the quiet middle child, then for a while the single uncle you couldn't really talk about. I know that was a challenge. At least now you know what I was up to for all those years. I am truly blessed to have such a wonderful family and be surrounded by your laughter, friendship, love and support.

And to Andrea, thank you for giving me another chance at a first date. I know I ask a lot of you. You kept my secrets, then you came and knocked on doors with me. You supported my career changes and the writing of this book, serving as my most trusted confidante and greatest source of encouragement, all the while being an amazing mother to our two wonderful children. You are my best friend, and I am so lucky to have you as my partner in life. I love you.

ABOUT THE AUTHOR

ANDREW KIRSCH was born and raised in Toronto, Ontario. He has a public policy degree from Brown University in Providence, Rhode Island, and worked as an investment advisor in London before serving for almost a decade at the Canadian Security Intelligence Service. He rose quickly from headquarters analyst to operational team lead in the special operations security unit, where he led covert entries into cars, homes and businesses to acquire sensitive information, plant listening devices and track targets of national security investigations.

After leaving CSIS, he was a founding member and first ever Department Security Officer in the Ontario Office of the Provincial Security Advisor (OPSA) with a mandate to enhance physical, personnel, information and network security across the Ontario Public Service.

He established Kirsch Consulting Group (KCG), a risk advisory firm composed of experienced, industry-leading practitioners from military, law enforcement, private investigation and intelligence backgrounds and cultivated from the national security community to help government, corporate and private clients secure their operations. KCG conducts physical and cyber security risk and vulnerability assessments and designs and assists in the implementation of strategic threat-mitigation solutions.

Kirsch ran in the 2018 Ontario provincial election in the Toronto-St. Paul's riding, where he lives with his wife and two young children.